Alexandra Orlando:
In Pursuit Of Victory

Martin Avery
with Alexandra Orlando

BookLand
press

TORONTO, CANADA

Published by:
Bookland Press Inc.
6021 Yonge Street
Suite 1010
Toronto, ON
Canada M2M 3W2
www.booklandpress.com

Printed and bound in Canada

Front cover photo by Grace Chiu
www.graceclick.com

Library and Archives Canada Cataloguing in Publication

Avery, Martin, 1955-
   Alexandra Orlando : in pursuit of victory / Martin Avery with Alexandra Orlando.

ISBN 0-9780838-2-2

   1. Orlando, Alexandra. 2. Rhythmic gymnastics--Canada.
3. Gymnasts--Canada--Biography. I. Orlando, Alexandra
II. Title.

GV460.2.O74A93 2006   796.44092   C2006-904931-9

Alexandra Orlando:
In Pursuit Of Victory

Alexandra The Great:
Canada's Rhythmic Gymnastics Champion
And Her Journey From The Magic Carpet
To The Podium
At The 2006 Commonwealth Games
For A Record-Setting
Six Gold Medals - And Beyond

Featuring:
profiles of rhythmic gymnastic champions
Lori Fung, Camille Martens,
Erika-Leigh Stirton,
Mary Sanders, and Maria Petrova

Plus
Dimitritchka "Mimi" Masleva,
rhythmic gymnastics coach for
Canada, Bulgaria, and Japan

And
Ritmika Rhythmic Gymnastics Club

Alexandra Orlando's Dedication

"If only I could get through this. God, God gotta help me get through this. I gotta get through this. I gotta get through this. I gotta make it, gonna make, gonna make it through."
~Daniel Bedingfield

I have come to this point in my life because I did make it through. I overcame the challenges and pushed on to achieve the unimaginable. But I didn't get through it alone. I am fortunate enough to have always been surrounded by the most amazing, generous, supportive people. Without them I wouldn't be where I am today and the woman I've become.

I want to firstly thank my family for their never-ending love and patience. How they deal with what I put them through on a daily basis is amazing. Mom, Dad, you are the greatest parents anyone could ask for. You just want me to be happy, which is how I keep sane in all this craziness. Whatever happens I know you'll be proud of me and that inspires me to go for my dreams. Victoria, I can't tell you in words what you mean to me. Growing up I wanted to be you. You are my hero, my role model, my light, my angel and always my big sister. I love you more than you know. To Grandma and my entire extended family in the US and Italy, I can feel your love and support wherever I go, always.

Thank you to my coach, Mimi Masleva, for pushing me to get the best performances out of myself. You've been there along the very bumpy ride, by my side helping me accomplish the unthinkable. I am honoured to have been able to work with you and look forward to sharing my ultimate goal together in Beijing.

Huge thanks goes to Annely Riga, Kairi Tirel and all coaches and members of Ritmika Rhythmic Gymnastics Club. Elvira Boudakova, you brought out the dancer in me and made me realize the passion I have inside myself. To all my teammates who have always been there for me and their families, who have supported and fundraised for me; people who have taken the time out of their very busy lives to not only care about their own daughters, but me as well - that is something incredible and I thank you all from the bottom of my heart.

I would also like to thank everyone in the gymnastics community across Canada who have been behind me since I was a little girl. When I compete I feel my country's pride wherever I am and that is because of the amazing support I have received over the past 15 years. Thank you to Jean Paul Caron, Gymnastics Canada; Slava Corn, Gymnastics Ontario; each and every provincial gymnastics federation; Blagovesta Ignatova, Danielle Frattarolli, head judges of Canada; Tamara Bompa and Wanda Ladyman; all the judges and coaches across Canada provincially and nationally; each and every rhythmic gymnast inspiring me to become their role model; every teammate, past and present, who experienced the world by my side and grew up together along the way; Kelly and Mary, we will always be the three musketeers; my fans; my role models; and I couldn't forget to thank all the Canadian athletes in all different sports who I've met along this incredible journey of mine, especially the men's and women's artistic teams, who have always been so supportive and cheered myself and our team on. Thanks guys, you are awesome to travel with and make competitions that much more fun. And last but not least, thank you to every rhythmic gymnastics club, especially Seneca, and Theresa Orr for always giving me the opportunity to use their wonderful facility this past year, and my former club Kalev, Mrs. Evelyn Koop, Svetlana Joukova and Ludmilla Dimitrova, for a great beginning to a long career.

This page wouldn't be complete without mentioning Sport Canada and the National Sport Center of Ontario for all they've done for me. As an athlete and student and teenage girl there are many obstacles I have to face on a daily basis. I am so grateful to be provided with numerous athletic professionals, all to help me progress. Thank you for making this incredible journey as smooth as possible. I would also like to thank the entire Fitness Institute, you are my second home; my trainer Chris Dalcin, for never giving up on me and becoming my very own sport psychologist; and my physiotherapist and miracle worker, Farhan Dhalla, for fixing me up whenever I'm broken.

Thank you to our family friends, who have taken me in and always treated me like their own daughter: the Marions, Hughs, Grahams, Sorbaras, Dietrichs, Palmays, Browns, Tanzolas, Connollys, Coutts, Eckhardts, Harlockers, Hartmanns and countless others. I would write a whole chapter on all of you if I could. Your support touches my heart.

Mercy, you are my other half; we are complete opposites, yet exactly alike. You know me better than anyone else in the world. Thank you for encouraging me to embrace each day with the calmness and serenity of a yoga instructor, the confidence of a super model, the intensity of a fighter pilot and the naive happiness of a child. I will never leave your side. We are soul sisters forever.

Although this paragraph is near the end of my very

long dedication page, you all are the most special people I know. Where would I be without my friends? You have stuck by me when I have cancelled on you, numerous times, vented, complained, cried and gone MIA. You are a select few that can deal with my kind of crazy life and calm me down when needed, which is often. You show me a side of myself where I can leave all my stress and worries at the door and be a normal teenager having some fun. Because of you I can experience the best of both worlds. Danielle you are my very own super star and let me escape to a fantasy world. Even when we think we've fallen apart we are always there for each other. To my girls that have stuck by me through high school and into University, who I can completely bare my soul to. In alphabetical order, so no one gets upset, ladies: Anna, Brianna, Duda, Jackie, Rita, Tiki and Veronica. I'd literally be lost if I didn't have you all in my life. Thank you to Isha, Leslie, Sarah, Katie, Amy, Marissa, Lindsay and Misha for being there for me when high school could've been a horrible place. I was lucky to be constantly surrounded by the most amazing girls at Havergal, there are just too many to even name, but you know who you are. I also wanted to thank those of you who I've known since I was a little girl twirling a ribbon for the first time. You supported me back then and never stopped. Amanda and Broidy, the support and friendship you've given me over the years means the world to me. As I enter this new era of my life I find myself surrounded by people that amaze me more and more everyday. Caye I wouldn't have gotten through first year alive if it wasn't for you. Who else synchronizes their iTunes together from literally one room away? I knew we would become best friends from the start. You helped me through one of the most difficult years of my life and I will never forget it. Thanks also to my 309 roomies, who put up with me all year, Adri, Helena and Kendall. To all the University of Toronto varsity swimmers I know (this was the easiest way to mention you all) thank you for making me an honorary team member. Brandon, what can I say? You have always been there for me and then some. Kass, Frankie and Marco, the high six will never go out of style (it had to be said). A huge thank you goes out to everyone I met during the year, especially at Woodsworth, New and St. Mike's, you made me believe I could be normal for a change. I have to thank all my sister's friends for putting up with the mention of rhythmic gymnastics and my name over and over and over; Kyle especially, you are the older brother I never had. If there is anyone I have forgotten to mention, I am extremely sorry, as you have all contributed to my success and my pursuit of victory in some way. I can't tell you how extremely hard it is to recall everyone in your life who has touched your heart. I guess that's a good thing. I love you all.

Thank you to my future boyfriend: no need to mention names here. For all of you reading this, you have just found out yet another surprising fact about Alexandra Orlando. Yes, I can make fun of myself and I thank all those people who do, too, because life isn't worth living if you're not continuously laughing, learning, and growing.

I want to thank Bookland Press for making this all possible. Robert Morgan and Martin Avery: I am in awe of your dedication to this project and your wonderful enthusiasm. Thank you for believing in me and telling my story to the world.

Lastly, I would like to thank Lori Fung for the beautifully written foreword. It is very humbling to hear someone like yourself speak of me in such a way. Your words are a comforting reminder that everything I have had to overcome has been for a reason and the best is most definitely yet to come.

I'll see you in Beijing at the 2008 Olympics!

Martin Avery's Dedication

To the rhythmic gymnast inside each of us and to our sisters.

"Ever try to toss a hoop up in the air and catch it on your foot? What about pitching two clubs in the air while executing a split leap and then re-grasping the clubs without knocking yourself out? Okay, here's a simple one - try rolling a ball across your chest from one end of your fingertips to the other. It looks and sounds easy but it's not. This is rhythmic gymnastics."

~ anon.

"I am a rhythmic gymnast. I am not an artistic gymnast or a figure skater, I do not train in an arena, or eat junk food, or own wrist guards. I don't know Miller, Tusek, or Moceanu, though I am certain they are really, really nice. I have ribbon, not beams, and I pronounce it "rhythmic" not "rhythm". I can proudly sew the club's logo on my track-suit. I believe in art and sport, not politics; hard work, not chance; and that the apparatus is an extension of your body. A rope is not a skipping rope, a hoop is not a hula-hoop. And it is OVER-splits, not split. Rhythmics is the all-time best sport."

~ anon.

Table of Contents

Foreword: Lori Fung, Canada's First Olympic
Medallist in Rhythmic Gymnastics............................. 16

Preface.. 20

1 Alexandra's Amazing Accomplishments
Against All Odds.. 22

2 Alexandra's Greatest Year - So Far...................... 29

3 The Quest For Victory, Medal-By-Medal And
Championship-By-Championship.......................... 35

4 Olympic Controversy And Challenges:
Imagine Coming "This Close" To Your Dream......... 42

5 Best Friends, Biggest Competitors: The
Alexandra And Mary Story...................................... 51

6 The Early Years Of Alex the Great........................ 61

7 Under The Influence: Mimi Masleva, Annely
Riga, Lori Fung, Camille Martens, Maria
Petrova, Erika-Leigh Stirton, The Family, and
Canada.. 74

8 Rhythmic Gymnastics Night In Canada (With
Coach's Corner Featuring Dimitritchka "Mimi"
Masleva)... 97

9 Diets And Disorders: Sacrificing Pizza, Pasta,
And Boyfriends... 111

10 High School Confidential: Woman's World............ 119

11 Varsity Freedom: Normal Life At Last.................... 125

12 Alex the Great And The Dangers Of

    Rhythmic Gymnastics... 128

13 Another Side Of Alex Orlando: An Insider's

    Report... 132

14 The Commonwealth Games Record-Setting

    Six Gold Medals.. 143

15 After The Gold.. 150

16 To The Olympics -- And Beyond!......................... 154

17 Secrets Of Success And A Few Words Of

    Advice... 171

    Martin Avery's Afterword.. 177

    *Appendix:*The Ultimate Guide To Rhythmic

    Gymnastics For Dummies And Idiots.................... 180

    Alexandra Orlando Rythmic Gymnastics Quiz........ 205

"The most important thing in the Olympic Games is not to win but to take part, just as the most important thing in life is not the triumph but the struggle. The essential thing is not to have conquered but to have fought well."

~ The Olympic Creed

Foreword By Lori Fung
Canada's First Olympic Gold Medallist In
Rhythmic Gymnastics

I watched Alex grow up and saw her win every national title in Canada - from novice through junior to senior - and I've judged her at competitions, so I would love to be a part of this book about Alexandra Orlando.

I feel so proud of her and not only as a gymnast but also as a role model. I've seen her work with the younger girls in rhythmic gymnastics, who idolize her, and it is great to see the way she interacts with them. She remains a real person, authentic and genuine, unlike so many who reach her level of success. She still takes the time to give a hug to a girl who is crying at a competition and to answer all the questions the novices and juniors are so excited to ask her.

I want to say to Alex that she's got what it takes to go all the way in rhythmic gymnastics. Of course, it also takes luck and timing. That's a huge part of any sport. She's taking care of the things she can control - training and competing at the right events - and she has something else everyone needs, in addition to her amazing gift for her sport.

I've met Alex's family - her parents and her sister - and I know they are supporting her in the best way. So much of my success in this sport, all the way to the Olympics, is due to my family, and Alex's family is just like mine. I've seen so many athletes with great potential ruined by overzealous parents. They push their kids too hard, they yell and scream at judges during competitions, and they make it all about winning or losing. Alex's family, like mine, is supportive no matter what the results are, if the scores given by judges are good or bad, or if you beat the competition or not. The ideal form of family support is encouragement to keep going and to be happy with what you are doing and that's it.

We put enough pressure on ourselves to perform extremely well in the most demanding circumstances. I worked so hard to get to the Olympics and I really wanted to do well when I got there, but I believe the reason I did so well, was that there was no pressure. I didn't know I would be going to the Olympics until five months before, so I didn't have a lot of time to worry about it. Expectations in Canada were not high. I felt free to enjoy my time there and performed as though I didn't have a care in the world. Many athletes turn in their worst performance at the Olympics because they feel enormous pressure. I felt relaxed and I won gold.

In those days, we did not compete in rhythmic gymnastics at the Pan American Games or the Commonwealth Games, so the Olympic Games was my very first multi-sport event. I thought it was the ultimate.

If Alex gets there, and I believe she will, I'm certain she will be inspired to turn in the best performance of her life - and that's really saying something. If that happens, who knows about the standings or medals?

If Alex had gone to the last Olympics, at such a young age, against that competition, it would have been a time for growing, as she was still very young and had much more growing to do as a gymnast. Alex was not at her peak at that time and I got the feeling it wasn't meant for her, that year. I talked to her during the time she was told she would be going and then wouldn't be going and she felt so disappointed. I told her to hang in there because it wasn't meant to be. She used that disappointment to her advantage, using the experience to inspire her to train harder, and that resulted in her amazing performance at the Commonwealth Games in Australia, winning all the gold, setting records, and being named Canada's flag-bearer.

Maybe the next Olympics are the Games that are meant to be for Alex. It will be a great experience.

I wish every athlete could have my experience. In those days, maybe I was naive, but I believed every judge was pulling for me. When I left the sport as a competitor, I was not bitter about the judging. I've given my whole life to this sport. I still love it, as a coach and as an international judge. It is a great sport for developing confidence, in addition to the athletic skills. I've seen many girls who have trained in Rhythmics, go from being completely introverted, to having the kind of confidence it takes to make it in the world outside of sports. Girls who were so shy that they could not look anyone in the eye have learned how to walk confidently into job interviews, and perform well under any kind of pressure. That kind of confidence cannot be learned just anywhere.

Alex has learned all about the technical part of rhythmic gymnastics but she also brings to the sport something, which cannot be taught by any coach. I didn't have the world's greatest technical skills, the incredible flexibility or the amazing jumps some gymnasts demonstrate, but artistry oozed out of me. That's a gift I was born with, and Alex has that gift, too.

When I watch Alex now, as a judge, it's hard for me to remember to concentrate like a judge because it is such a pleasure to watch her perform. I just want to sit back and enjoy the show. She has the technical skills and a lot more. Many rhythmic gymnasts from other countries develop the skills but perform them like robots. They are too robotic in their presentation. Alex has an amazing ability to express personality in her performances and that is what really characterizes our sport. The way Alex does her magic on that carpet makes the hairs at the back of your neck stand up.

Alex the Great is amazing.

Note: The Canadian athlete Lori Fung was the first rhythmic gymnast in the world to win Olympic gold. Lori Fung Methorst, CM, OBC, is now a retired rhythmic gymnast and an active gymnastics judge. At the 1984 Summer Olympics, in Los Angeles, she won the first gold medal ever awarded for the sport of rhythmic gymnastics. She went on to coach for the Canadian National Team, the USA National Team, and the Mexican National Team. She is currently a consultant for Club Elite Rhythmics in British Columbia. She is also known for the part she played as an aerial ballerina in the film Catwoman. By the time she retired in 1988, she had claimed not only the Olympic gold medal, but seven Canadian National Senior titles from 1982-1988 and four Four Continent All Around titles. She has been inducted into the British Columbia Hall of Fame, and the Canadian Sports Hall of Fame. She is also a member of the Order of British Columbia and the Order of Canada.

Preface

Alexandra Orlando: *In Pursuit Of Victory*, the first book in the new series about Canadian athletes by *BookLand Press*, is the story of the rhythmic gymnast who set a world record by winning six gold medals at the 2006 Commonwealth Games in Australia, and now has her sights set on the 2008 Olympic Games.

Alex the Great, as she is known to her family, has had the Olympic dream since she was seven and discovered she loved competing in rhythmic gymnastics. She came incredibly close to realizing her dream at the last Olympic Games, as she was hoping for a spot and then had her hopes taken away by the international politics of the Olympics in her sport.

Rhythmic gymnastics is a marriage of music, dance, and gymnastic floor routines using apparatus and it is not nearly as popular in Canada as it is in Europe, where Alexandra Orlando is considered a superstar. Coming from Canada, where her sport is relatively new, Alex has had to overcome incredible odds to join the elite of rhythmic gymnastics internationally.

She is the reigning Canadian champion, our national champion for the past five years, and the number one rhythmic gymnast in North America.

Alex's chosen sport is very demanding in terms of strength, endurance, flexibility, balance, and coordination, and competitors have to look beautiful, too, with sequined and crystal costumes rivaling the outfits designed for figure skaters. The emphasis on appearance has led to eating disorders in the teams from countries that dominate the sport.

Alex has overcome her battles with diets and size and is ready to take on the leaders of her sport, who may look too thin to be healthy. Beautiful, strong, with great muscle tone and zero body fat, looking very healthy, from an incredible number of hours training and working out, Alex is ready to take on the world. At 20, she is poised to peak just in time for the next Olympics. She has cracked the top 15 internationally and is moving in on the top ten. Could her pursuit of victory lead to an Olympic medal for Canada in 2008?

Chapter 1: Alexandra's Amazing Accomplishments Against All Odds

Can a Canadian kid make it to the Olympics for rhythmic gymnastics?

Alexandra Orlando is overcoming all the obstacles and great odds in her pursuit of victory. She comes from a country without the best training facilities, no popular support for her sport, little financial support, and without a longstanding tradition of excellence in rhythmic gymnastics, but she has already experienced great international success, with gold medal performances at the Pan-Am Games, Commonwealth Games, and many others, she has cracked the top 15 in the world for her sport, is already considered number one in the most important part of her sport, and it looks as though she is on her way to the 2008 Olympic Games in Beijing.

The Alexandra Orlando Story: Challenges And Victories

The Alexandra Orlando story is filled with stellar accomplishments but it is also about turning disappointments into challenges and victories. It is a Cinderella story, about overcoming great odds and having dreams come true. It is also a very Canadian story.

At age 19, Alexandra The Great, as she is known to her family, had an amazing year, after an awe-inspiring 14-year career in rhythmic gymnastics. Now, at age 20, she is aiming even higher.

After winning a record six gold medals at the 2006 Commonwealth Games, and also earning the honour of being named Canada's flag-bearer in the closing ceremonies of those Commonwealth Games in Australia, this young woman instantly became the most recognizable rhythmic gymnastics star since Lori Fung won gold in the sport's Olympic debut in 1984 at Los Angeles. Alexandra went on to become our national champion for the fifth straight year and then cracked the top 15 in her sport internationally. Many say she is already number one in the world at ribbon, which is a key element of rhythmic gymnastics. She has her eyes on an even bigger prize: the 2008 Olympics.

The question is: How does she do it?

Is it a gift or does she have to work hard? What are the secrets of her success in this incredibly competitive sport? Why didn't she leave Canada and go to the USA to compete? How will she do at the Olympics?

Clearly, Alexandra is a gifted gymnast. But she does train incredibly hard. And, like Cinderella, she has had to face many challenges, including: training for many years in inadequate facilities without government support; overcoming the politics of judging; dealing with the disappointment of coming so close to an Olympic birth but getting cut at the last minute; profound pressures in high school; eating disorders all around her in her sport; dealing with newfound fame and superstar status in Europe; her neglected and misunderstood sport at home in Canada and the rest of North America; being overshadowed by winter sports - especially hockey - in Canada; trying to understand how her best friend could turn into her biggest competitor; withstanding the temptation and offers to train in the USA and compete for the Americans instead of against them; competing against highly trained, well-paid, rhythmic gymnasts from countries in Europe that build palaces to the sport and support it in every way; not to mention sacrificing pizza, pasta, chocolate, boyfriends, and romance, in order to make room for her passion for her sport and her desire to go from doing her magic on the carpet all the way to the podium at the major competitions in the world.

The Alexandra Orlando story is about a girl who had the Olympic dream from a very early age, came incredibly close to realizing it at age 17, turned her disappointment into a dominating performance for Canada at the Commonwealth Games, and is now aiming at the Olympics again.

She is truly Canadian and, therefore, modest and self-effacing, but she is proud of her club, her sport, her accomplishments, and her country, so you can call her Alexandra The Great, if you like. After all, that's what her father calls her. He's her biggest fan. But you better check with her mom, because she's Alex's manager.

This is the story of the Alexandra Orlando support system, as well as of Alex, as that is at the top of the list of her secrets to success.

To be a rhythmic gymnast, you must be a true all around athlete. Those in the know say rhythmic gymnastics is truly the hardest sport. It has been said that in order to be a rhythmic gymnast you must throw, catch, and leap with precision, like Michael Jordan; you must be as strong as Popeye and as flexible as Gumby; have the heart of a dancer and the soul of an artist; and the flexibility of a contortionist as well as the strength and courage of a marathon runner.

The competition is incredible, especially from the former countries of the Soviet Union, where governments have erected palaces to this sport. The golden girls of rhythmic gymnastics are regarded as superstars in their countries and around the world, Alex and her coach report. They are paid well to focus on their training and competitions, given some of the greatest coaches available, for one-on-one training, and frequently face serious competition locally. And in those places, rhythmic gymnastics seems to be in the blood, the way hockey is in Canada.

In Eastern Europe and the former Soviet countries, Canada's national rhythmic gymnastics champion, Alexandra Orlando, is already a superstar. Everyone knows her name. Fans collect photographs and posters, stand in line for her autograph, and follow her career, from competition to competition, as she progresses from European events to World Championships and heads - again - toward the Olympics.

In places where they follow her sport closely, Alex is loved the way Canadians love their own female ice hockey stars.

"Alexandra has already done amazing things, breaking into the top 15 internationally," says her coach, Dimitritchka "Mimi" Masleva, formerly of Bulgaria and Japan.

"If there was just one team representing all the former Soviet countries, as in my era, Alex would already be in the top ten in the world and would be moving in on the top three in time for the next Olympics," she claims.

Annely Riga, the president of Ritmika, the club where Alex trains, says, "She is already the best in the world in "ribbon", which is the key event in her competitions."

The rules of her sport have recently changed, to Alex's advantage, and the policies of the Canadian Olympic Commission have also changed, so they can help her. She is now a carded athlete, getting financial support from her country. Also, she is peaking physically at just the right time for the next Olympic Games. It seems all the stars are aligning for

Alexandra Orlando's pursuit of victory.

"The Russians used to shake their heads in amazement at Alex's success," her coach says, "because they knew we had no training facility in Canada, as they do in Russia, and Alex's parents or her club was sending her to competitions, rather than her home country."

Mimi Masleva shakes her head sadly at the memory. "If I could work one-on-one with Alex, exclusively, the way the Russians do it, with one coach for one athlete," she says, "Alex would be ten times better and several steps ahead of where she is now, so she would be ready to take on the very best in the world."

Without sponsors, without the use of the best facilities in the world, or even in Canada, a country which has no venue dedicated to her sport, and sharing her coach with dozens of other athletes in training, not to mention her job at Seneca College, Alex would have enough obstacles, but she is also attending classes at the University of Toronto, has to travel from her school in downtown Toronto to Ritmika, her club, located in Vaughan, north of Toronto, an hour away, to train, and has to compete against girls with smaller builds, favoured by the judges in her sport.

Alex is not a waif, like some of the Eastern European women who are in the top ten internationally in rhythmic gymnastics. She is taller, more muscular, bigger. However, she performs in the fiery, flowing, passionate style the Bulgarians made famous, and it suits her body type. She looks beautiful on the rhythmic gymnastics carpet, moves gracefully, and has remarkable presence.

"She has a spark," the president of her club says. "She has that spark and also the ability to project it."

"She has great presence," her mom admits. "Alex

shows real fire out there, on the carpet. She has great passion and her spirit really shows. The Bulgarian style suits her and she suits it. Their movements flow with the music beautifully."

"She performs with real fire and is beautiful to watch," her coach says.

"Alex is amazing," says Ritmika president Annely Riga. "She is passionate about rhythmic gymnastics and you cannot do this sport at such a high level without passion."

How has she overcome all these odds to find so much success in her sport?

"Alex was born with great energy and a desire for recognition," her mother notes, "She discovered a love of competition as soon as she got into the competitive stream of rhythmic gymnastics, at a very young age, and she has never quit or stopped training harder and harder."

Orlando relies on her strength, incredible speed, and apparatus technique to perform the quadruple turns and high throws that win her the top points. She stands out at a more superficial level, too, wearing her long hair in a simple bun and using restrained amounts of make-up, by rhythmic gymnastics standards.

Paul Orlando, Alex's father says, "It's what she's striving for and it's unbelievable what she can do in competition. She works better under stress; it gets the adrenaline going, and then she can do truly unbelievable things."

Orlando's coach, Mimi Masleva says she believes her brightest pupil can continue to improve in the elite competitions ruled by Russians, Bulgarians, and Belorussians.

"Her outstanding performance at the 2006 Commonwealth Games in Australia will serve as a valuable confidence boost and it gives her some momentum for a spot at the 2008 Olympic Summer Games in China," Annely Riga says. She is the owner of the Ritmika, the rhythmic gymnastics club where Orlando has trained since 1998.

Alexandra deals with disappointments - from small ones, such as the politics of judging, to enormous ones, including getting left out of the last Olympics - by training harder and at a higher level of difficulty, never losing her love of the sport or her gift for expressing the passion she feels through the combination of dancing in gorgeous costumes and the incredible athleticism, which is what the sport we call rhythmic gymnastics is all about.

"She touches you with every movement," her coach says.

Can this Canadian athlete make it in the elite world of competitive international rhythmic gymnastics? The answer to that question is: This is Alexandra Orlando, *in pursuit of victory.*

Chapter 2: Alexandra's Greatest Year - So Far

Alexandra The Great had the most amazing year in 2006, after an awe-inspiring 14-year career in rhythmic gymnastics. The Alexandra Orlando story is filled with stellar accomplishments. But it is also a story about turning huge disappointments and challenges into victories by working harder and harder and training at higher and higher levels.

So far, newspaper headlines around the world have told her story: "Alexandra The Great", "Orlando Blooms", and "Alexandra Orlando Wins Every Gold Available In The Rhythmic Gymnastics."

She is most famous for creating Commonwealth Games history by winning gold medals in every discipline in the rhythmic gymnastics competitions. Alex is the first woman to claim six gold medals in the sport, at the Commonwealth Games. She earned gold individually for the rope, ball, ribbon and clubs, and for "Team" and "All Round". Her half-dozen gold medals equals the record at a single Games - another remarkable feat.

At age 19, she surpassed her Canadian hero, Erika-Leigh Stirton, who took home five gold medals at the 1998 Commonwealth Games in Kuala Lumpur, to become the greatest rhythmic gymnast in the history of Canada at the Commonwealth Games.

How did she do that?

The year after she lost her first chance to go to the

Olympic Games, Alex turned her disappointment into a tour de force display of athleticism and showmanship at the 2006 Commonwealth Games in Australia. She wowed the sold-out crowd, the judges, and TV audiences around the world, for three straight days in Melbourne. It was a clean sweep of the all around and individual events for rope, ribbon, ball and clubs, and a victory in the team event.

That scintillating performance matched the Commonwealth Games record for gold medals, shared by Canada's Graham Smith, who had six gold medals in swimming at the 1978 Commonwealth Games in Edmonton, and Australian swim stars Ian Thorpe and Susie O'Neill. It is a very exclusive club.

When she won all six rhythmic gymnastics events included as part of the gymnastics program at the 2006 Commonwealth Games in Melbourne, she joined a very small group of elite athletes. Graham Smith, the Canadian swimmer, won his six gold medals back in 1978, when the Commonwealth Games were held in Edmonton. Susie O'Neill, from Australia, won six gold medals in the swimming pool in 1998, when the Commonwealth Games were held in Kuala Lumpur. Ian Thorpe, another Australian swimmer, equaled O'Neill's feat in 2002, at the Commonwealth Games in Manchester, England. They are the only competitors to win six gold medals at a single Commonwealth Games. That's the kind of athlete Alexandra Orlando is.

Overnight Sensation

It seemed as though Alexandra Orlando emerged on the international scene suddenly, like an overnight sensation, but she had been in pursuit of victory for over a decade.

Before her incredible accomplishments at the

Commonwealth Games in Australia, Alex had already won every rhythmic gymnastics event at the Canadian National Championships for three years in a row. She was Canada's national champion in 2003, 2004 and 2005.

Immediately after the closing ceremonies in Melbourne, where she was Canada's flag-bearer, Alex had good news for rhythmic gymnastics in Canada: instead of retiring from rhythmic gymnastics, going out while on the top, she was setting her sights on the Olympics in Beijing in 2008.

Alexandra Orlando thoroughly dominated at the 18th Commonwealth Games.

When she carried the Canadian flag into the closing ceremonies at the Melbourne Cricket Ground, she instantly became the standard-bearer for her sport. In Canada, she is its most recognizable star in her sport since Lori Fung of Vancouver won gold in the sport's Olympic debut in 1984 at Los Angeles.

At the 2006 Commonwealth Games, Alexandra helped Canada win the team event, then mopped the floor in the all-round event, picking up the gold medals in all the individual apparatus finals, one after the other: the rope, the ball, the clubs, the ribbon. She scored top marks in all four disciplines and finished the championship with 59.150 points out of a possible 80.

The Commonwealth Games star continued her winning ways when she went home, capturing the all-around title at the Canadian rhythmic gymnastics championships in Surrey, BC, shortly after returning to Canada from Australia.

Her goal for the following season was to break into the top 15 in rhythmic gymnastics internationally and then move into the top ten in time for the Olympics.

Just Alex

Despite her phenomenal success, Alexandra remains rooted, grounded, and balanced. She is as humble as the stereotypical Canadian, and that is appropriate as she is Canadian through and through.

What did Alex have to say after all that success? She told reporters it felt "unreal" and said she hoped her six medal performance and all the attention it got would boost the popularity of rhythmic gymnastics in Canada and inspire people to take it more seriously. That was her concern.

Not many people even know what rhythmic gymnastics is, she told reporters.

"I had an amazing year," Alex says.

She is modest and understated in the well-known Canadian manner, but how else can you describe a year like this?

Alex is now ranked 15th, internationally.

"I've traveled to France a dozen times, and I've been to Germany, England, Portugal, Spain, Bulgaria, Russia, Ukraine, Azerbaijan... and Australia," she says. "The crowds at rhythmic gymnastics competitions in some of those places are like hockey fans in Canada. There are lots of spectators and serious fans. People scream in the audience, boo the judges, and show they understand the intricacies of the sport. In some places, they sell my picture for 15 Euros, make posters for sale, and recognize me wherever I go. It always amazes me that people know who I am. I'm a humble Canadian. I'm not embarrassed to talk about my successes but I don't feel they've changed me. I'm still me. Some people call me Alex the Great, but I'm really the same Alexandra I've always been."

"It's hard for me to think of myself as a famous person and I can't stand it when I'm introduced as "the winner of six gold medals at the Commonwealth games and the four-time national champion". Sometimes my friends say things like that just to tease me."

"My dad is the one who started calling me Alex the Great and it caught on at the Commonwealth Games."

Her biggest complaint about the Commonwealth Games in Australia?

"There have been a lot of headlines around the world saying "Orlando Blooms". I felt that got old real fast."

Aside from that, it is apparent she loved every minute of her time in Melbourne.

"My mom saw me on the Jumbotron," Alex recalls. "She was on the other side of the stadium from the podium where I was presented my six gold medals. The four-hour - long closing ceremonies were amazing and the Australian organizers were so good to us. The Commonwealth Games Canada committee helped us out a lot, too, by getting seats for parents, quickly, but they couldn't get my mom close enough to take pictures. In fact, I have no pictures of that moment. There were millions of pictures taken and I've been given lots of pictures of myself in other places but I have no photos of that golden moment!"

At the Commonwealth Games, rhythmic gymnastics was the most popular sport with other athletes, Alex reports. "They all wanted to watch rhythmic gymnastics. The spring show at my club is very popular, too. In Europe, we compete in front of huge crowds. When we come back, we perform in front of the usual crowd, in Canada, which is made up primarily of our parents. It's disappointing. But we had good crowds for the Nationals, this year. So things are improving. I'd rather have a huge crowd."

Unchanged By Phenomenal Success

"I feel normal, even though I don't live a normal life," she says. "I think of myself as just Alex, another student at University of Toronto. I'm humble, like a typical Canadian. I don't go around telling people I'm a national champion or award-winning gymnast. I usually tell people I do gymnastics and let it go at that."

"Friends say I should be proud and talk about it more. I want to be known as me, not just as the four-time national champion who won gold six medals at the Commonwealth Games."

"I haven't changed, even though I've got a lot of attention from the media, lately. I've had my picture in a lot of newspapers. But I'm still me. What you see is what you get."

"Winning is personal, for Alex," her father explains. "It's not something she does for other people. That's the way Alex approaches it."

He adds, "We're here to support her if she loses and when she wins."

Her cool, calm, collected approach to life does not reveal any of her secrets to success in the incredibly competitive world of rhythmic gymnastics at the most elite level. It appeared as though a quiet Canadian burst onto the international scene like an overnight sensation. Could it be? Or did she put together her victory methodically over the years, step-by-step, piece-by-piece, medal-by-medal, event-by-event, and championship-by-championship?

Who was it who said, "It took me years and years of hard work to be an overnight sensation"?

Chapter 3: The Quest For Victory, Medal-By-Medal And Championship-By-Championship

Alexandra Orlando burst onto the international scene as the winner of a record-setting six gold medals at the Commonwealth Games and as Canada's flag-bearer at the closing ceremonies. She was just 19-years-old.

She went from the carpet to that podium, again and again, by climbing up from being Canadian Novice National Champion, to junior National Champion, to Junior Pan American Champion, to Canadian Senior National Champion, to Commonwealth champion.

For millions of sports fans, Alex the Great may have appeared to have been an overnight sensation, bursting onto the scene with her megawatt smile lighting up the Jumbotron, but rhythmic gymnastics fans around the world have had the pleasure of watching her rise to the occasion, step-by-step, for a decade, winning national and international competitions, before arriving at the Commonwealth Games.

Here's how she did it, year-by-year, event-by-event, medal-by-medal, championship-by-championship, from Novice Canadian to Commonwealth Champion, becoming one of the top competitors in the world.

Alexandra came into prominence in her sport quite early. At just 12-years-old, she swept the all around and individual title in the novice competition of the 1999 Canadian Championships.

During her 14-year career as a rhythmic gymnast,

Orlando has won countless competitions. Here's a short list of her best results this century:

- 2000 Junior Pan American Games, Venezuela: 1st All-around, 1st with ball, 3rd with team;
- 2000 Canadian Junior Championships: 1st All-around;
- 2000 International of Schmiden, Germany: 6th All-around, 1st with hoop;
- 2000 Coupe d'Opale, Calais, France: 3rd All-around;
- 2003 Canadian Championships: 1st All-around;
- 2000 International of Portimao, four golds, AA and all finals;
- 2001 Canadian Junior Championships: 1st All-around;
- 2001 Four Continents Championships, Curitiba, Brazil: 2nd All-around;
- 2002 Berlin World Cup: 21st All-around;
- 2002 Canadian Championships: 2nd All-around;
- 2002 Pacific Alliance Championships, Burnaby: 3rd All-around, 2nd with team;
- 2002 Tournament of Corbeil-Essones, France: 36th All-around;
- 2003 Canadian Championships: 1st All-around;
- 2003 Berlin Masters, Germany: 22nd All-around;
- 2003 Tournament of Corbeil-Essones, France: 31st All-around;
- 2003 Zhulietta Shishmanova Memorial, Bulgaria: 7th All-around;
- 2003 Moscow Grand Prix: 21st All-around;
- 2004 Canadian Rhythmic Gymnastics Champion;
- 2004 Pacific Alliance winner with four Silver and one Bronze medal;
- 2006 Commonwealth Games, Australia: Six gold medals;
- 2006 Elite Canada, ranked 1st AA, 1st in rope, ball, clubs, and ribbon.

The full list of her accomplishments is nothing short of astounding, beginning with her early years.

Alexandra started Recreational Rhythmics when she was five-years-old and started competing at the Provincial Level at age eight. From the beginning, she always placed in the top four.

In her second year of competing at the Provincial level, she was First Overall at the Kanata Cup, at the Etobicoke Olympium, the Ritmika Invitational, the Niagara Challenge, and Provincial Qualifiers.

At age nine, she came 2nd Overall at the Provincial Championships with 1st place in Rope.

At age ten, she started competing at National Level.

In 1997, she was 6th Overall at Elite Ontario, 4th Overall at Eastern Regionals, and 4th Overall at National Championships.

The next year, she was 2nd Overall and 1st on Rope at the Questo Invitational; 3rd Overall with a 1st in Ball, 2nd in Hoop, and 3rd in Rope at Elite Ontario; 2nd Overall at the Eastern regionals; and 3rd Overall, with a 1st in Hoop and 2nd in Rope at the National Championships.

In 1999, Alexandra was the Novice Ontario Champion at the Elite Ontario Championships and the Novice National Champion at Montreal Nationals.

The year 2000 was a big year for Alexandra as she became Junior National Champion, with a 1st in Hoop and Rope and a 2nd in Clubs and Ball and then she started competing internationally.

She was 6th Overall at Fellbach-Schmiden, with a 1st in Hoop and 2nd in Ball, and took 3rd Overall as a Junior at Coupe D'Opale with a 3rd in Hoop, 4th in Ball and Clubs, and 5th in Rope.

She was 1st All-around at Elite Ontario, 1st All-around at Portugal Invitational, with four gold medals in finals, and 1st All-around at National Championships in Edmonton, with four gold medals in finals.

She took 4th place at an international competition in Bulgaria.

A longer list of her accomplishments would also include these remarkable achievements:

- 2000: Junior Pan American Championships, San Felipe, Venezuela All-around Champion, Gold in Ball, Silver in Rope, Hoop, Clubs;
- 2001: Four Continents Championships (Brazil): Silver Junior All-around, Silver in Ball, Clubs, Bronze in Hoop, and Ribbon;
- 2001 National Championships: Gold Junior All-around, Hoop, Ball, Clubs, Ribbon; Alexandra is the junior national Champion;
- 2001 Elite Ontario Gold Junior All-around, Hoop, Ball, Clubs, Ribbon;
- 2001 Portimao, Portugal. Bronze Junior All-around;
- 2001 Elite Canada All-around Junior Champion, Gold in Ball, Clubs, Hoop;
- 2002 Berlin World Cup: 21st place;
- 2002 National Championships (Calgary): 2nd place, giving her a position on the Canadian National Team;
- 2002 Corbeil-Essonnes (France): 36th place in her first major international competition as a Senior (out of 76 competitors);
- 2002 Pacific Alliance (British Columbia) Bronze Senior All-around, Bronze in ball, clubs, 4th place in hoop and rope;
- 2002: Ontario Elite: Silver in Senior All-around;
- 2002: Elite Canada Competition: Silver in Senior All-

around, number 2 National Team member.

In 2003 at the World Championships, in Budapest, Hungary, Alex claimed 23rd place in qualification round All-around, 16th place in All-around finals, and 9th place in Clubs. At the Levski Cup in Sofia, Bulgaria, Alex took 7th place. At the Vitry Cup in Zaragoza, Spain, she took 18th place. At the Queen Margarita international competition in Bulgaria, she took 4th in the All-around, 1st in Hoop, 2nd in Clubs, 6th in Ball, 8th in Ribbon. In the finals, she was 4th in Hoop, Clubs, and Ribbon, and 7th in Ball. Alex also won the prize for being named 'Favourite Gymnast of the Competition'.

At the Pan American Games, in Santo Domingo, Dominican Republic, Alex won three silver medals, in hoop, clubs, ribbon, plus a bronze in ball. Alex described her ribbon routine as "the best of her life". She came 6th in the All-around.

Alexandra dropped one spot from her day one finish, to 6th place. The competition was won by Mary Sanders, a dual citizen of Canada and the USA, competing for the USA.

In the group event, Canada earned a bronze for their ribbon routine and silver for hoops and balls. Brazil scored 49.650 points to take the gold medal, with Canada scoring 42.600 points and taking the silver medal over Cuba with 37.300 points.

At the Berlin Grand Prix she took 22nd place in All-around. At the Canada's National Championships, she was named Canadian National Champion with five gold medals. At the Corbeil-Essonnes International Grand Prix, she was in 31st place in the All-around.

At the Julieta Shishmanova international competition in Bulgaria, she took 7th place All-around and was 6th in both hoop and ball. At Elite Ontario, she took 1st place and became Ontario's 2003 Champion. At the Quebec Invitational, held in

Montreal, she took 1st place. At Elite Canada (Edmonton) 1st All-around, Gold in all finals, 2003 Canadian Champion. At the Moscow Grand Prix, she took 19th place.

In 2004, at the Shishmanova competition, in Bulgaria, Alexandra won bronze in ribbon, came 6th in All-around, 2nd in ribbon, 4th in Clubs, 5th in Ball, and 6th in Hoop.

At the Pacific Alliance Championships in Hawaii, in the All-around competition, Alex came 3rd. In the apparatus finals, she won four silvers. At Elite Ontario, Alexandra won the Ontario Championships. At the Thiais Grand Prix, Alex came 15th. At the Deriugina Cup, in Kiev, Ukraine, at the NAFTOGRAZ Grand Prix, she was 15th in the All-around. Taking out extra gymnasts per country, that would have left Alex in 10th place. At Elite Canada, Alex came 1st in all four apparatus, and 1st overall.

Competition Highlights

In 1999, Alexandra was Canada's Novice National Champion. In 2000, she was Pan American Junior Champion and Canada's Junior National Champion. In 2001, she was the Four Continents Junior Champion and Canada's Junior National Champion.

In 2002, she was a Senior Silver medallist. In the 2003 Pan-American Games, she won three silver medals and one bronze medal, which was good for 6th place AA. She was also the 2003 Canadian Rhythmic Gymnastics Champion.

Orlando has swept to win every rhythmic gymnastics event at the Canadian National Championships in 2003, 2004 and 2005. Alex has been the reigning Canadian Rhythmic Gymnastics Champion since 2003. At the World Championships in 2003, she took 16th place. Alex was 9th in clubs and the Canadian team was 19th in clubs during the All-around finals.

In 2004, she was Canadian Rhythmic Gymnastics Champion and also the 2004 Pacific Alliance winner with four silver and one bronze medal.

In 2005, she was Canadian Rhythmic Gymnastics Champion, winning five gold medals. As well as being National Champion, she was named the #1 National Team member.

At the 2005 World Championships, in Baku, Azerbaijan, Alexandra placed 18th in the individual all-around competition out of 125 competitors from 47 countries. The Canadian Team placed 14th out of 31 countries. Two years earlier, the Canadians placed 19th. This was one of the strongest Canadian Team results ever.

At the 2005 Elite Canada competition, Alexandra swept gold in all apparatus: Rope, Ball, Clubs, and Ribbon, and nobody could beat that so she was also 1st overall.

In 2006, she was awarded a World Class Gymnast Recognition award by the International Federation of Gymnastics.

In 2006, she was the Commonwealth Games Champion with six gold medals. In that same year, she was the Canadian Rhythmic Gymnastics Champion and at Elite Canada 2006 she was ranked 1st AA, after coming 1st in rope, ball, clubs, and ribbon. She was also the Commonwealth Games flag bearer for Canada.

At the Elite Canada 2006 event in Montreal, Alexandra Orlando was 1st AA, 1st in rope, ball, clubs, and ribbon.

And that's how you become an overnight sensation, winning six gold medals at the Commonwealth Games, a major international event with TV coverage around the world.

Chapter 4. Olympic Controversy And Challenges: Imagine Coming "This Close" To Your Dream

"Fifty years ago, for five minutes you came within... y-you came this close. It would KILL some men to get so close to their dream and not touch it. God, they'd consider it a tragedy."
~ Ray Kinsella to Moonlight Graham in *Field Of Dreams* (based on Shoeless Joe, by W.P. Kinsella)

The newspaper headlines of the time told the whole story: "Olympic Defeat", "RHYTHMIC GYMNASTICS DEALT A BLOW AS ORLANDO DENIED OLYMPIC BERTH", and "the highest-ranked athlete in the world not invited to participate at the Games".

Alexandra Orlando, Canada's best rhythmic gymnast, was denied the opportunity to compete at the Olympic Games when the International Olympic Committee awarded the final Olympic berth. She was bitterly disappointed after being denied the opportunity to compete at the 2004 Summer Olympics in Athens. She had hoped to gain entry to that competition as one of two wild-card exemptions the rhythmic gymnastics federation permits. Twenty were chosen; Alex was number 21. She was named the North American alternate for the Olympics, but the alternate did not get to go to the big show that year.

"Some people said not going to the Olympics was better for Alex than going and flopping, but I'm sure that she would be fine, once she got there," Marisa Orlando says. "Competition brings out her best. Who knows how well she would have done at those Olympics? When there are only 30 competitors, Alex really shines. At events where only two per country are allowed to compete, the odds are better for Alex."

The IOC determined that the final competitive berth, known as the Tripartite Commission wild card, would be awarded to Vania Vicente Monteiro of Cape Verde. The other continental wild cards were awarded several months earlier by the International Gymnastics Federation to athletes from Africa, Australia, and Great Britain, based on qualification results.

"Alex was never promised an Olympic spot," her mother explains. "She had to place 20th and she placed 21st in the qualifier and 16th in the overall competition, but the Canadian Olympic Committee wouldn't have sent her any-way as you had to be top 12. We were fighting for the wild card but at that point it was very political."

As a result of the decision, Canada would not be rep-resented in rhythmic gymnastics for the first time since the sport's inclusion in the Olympic Games in 1984.

"Alex was ranked 21st, at one point, before those Olympics, and the top 20 were supposed to go," Marisa Orlando explains. "In rhythmic gymnastics, the top 150 go to the "Worlds", and the top 20 go to the Olympics."

The decision has further frustrated Orlando's support-ers because it meant that two athletes from the continent of Africa would be competing in the Games, both based on wild cards. In contrast, all of the Americas, both North America and South America, would only have one representative. That one athlete was Mary Sanders, the former Canadian champion who elected to use her dual citizenship to represent the United

States. She was also Alex's best friend, like a sister, and her training partner at her club, Ritmika, in Toronto. Both athletes shared the same coach, Mimi Masleva. Alex was named as Mary's alternate. As the official alternate for rhythmic gymnastics, she would have the chance to compete, should a qualified country elect not to compete.

"The time leading up to the Olympics was very exciting and challenging," Marisa Orlando explains. "Week-by-week, day-by day, doors were opening and it looked as though Mary and then Alexandra, too, would have the chance to go to the Olympics, representing Canada."

"Mary placed 8th at the World Championships that year, which was unexpected," her coach says.

In light of the fact that Africa had already been awarded a wild card by the FIG, Canadian officials were hopeful that the IOC would not exercise their right to use the Tripartite wild card. The wild card would then have been returned to the FIG, who would have awarded it to the next-highest ranking athlete not in the Games. Ranked 21st in Olympic qualifying, Orlando would have been the next athlete in line for the FIG wild card, and would be the highest-ranked athlete in the world not invited to participate at the Olympic Games.

"It's a very complicated and confusing process," Marisa Orlando says. "Twenty-five competitors from around the world get to go to the Olympics for rhythmic gymnastics. Ten come from qualifying countries, based on international standings and qualifying competitions, and then every continent is represented. That year, North America was under-represented and Africa was over-represented, in my opinion."

At the previous year's world championships, Orlando finished 16th All-around. She was also the defending Canadian national champion and two-time defending Elite

Canada champion.

"Not sending her, although she qualified, was hard to take," her father says. "It's like a business decision. I felt it was wrong because she worked so hard to get there."

Marisa Orlando expressed disappointment with the decision.

"We knew that Cape Verde fit the bill regarding a very small delegation," Orlando said, "but the athlete in question placed 106th at world championships, which in our mind, did not fit the bill. Also, Africa already has a continent wild card and we were surprised that they would get another one."

Rhythmic Gymnastics Canada president Adrienne Arnold agreed with Marisa Orlando. Arnold noted that the African continent had already been awarded a "wild card" by the FIG, to cover the necessary "universality" issue. She said FIG and the IOC should have compared notes to consider the implications of a country of the same continent being award-ed the Tripartite card.

Many believed North and South America should have been better represented at the Olympics in Greece instead of Africa, that Canada should have been represented instead of Cape Verde, with Alexandra Orlando, who was ranked 21st instead of Wania Monteiro who was ranked 105th.

For Orlando and the rest of the Canadian gymnastics community, the decision came as a surprise. Monteiro ranked last in the previous year's Olympic qualification. The Tripartite Wild Card was designed to encourage participation for smaller countries, with fewer than six athletes qualified to the Olympic Games, provided that the athlete meets a required technical standard. Monteiro finished 106th at the last world championships, which made Canadian and other officials wonder whether she met the technical standards needed to compete at the Olympic Games.

"We were climbing the walls, getting the message that Canada was going, one day, and not going, the next, back and forth, until we felt we were going crazy. It was very hard on Alex and for our whole club."

"The year before the 2004 Olympics was very hard on all of us. It was a roller-coaster ride with many big ups and downs for Alex, her coach, her club, and her family. It was hard for the mom to keep going. I felt like quitting."

"Alex never thought about quitting for long. At the start of each season, we said to her, "If you're going to start this season, you have to finish it. You can't quit in the middle." She always gave us a look that said, "I'll never quit.""

"Even if Alex was 20th, we would have had to deal with the Canadian Olympic Committee, as they had decided to support only those athletes who were in the top 12 in their sport internationally. They thought that was the best way for Canada to get medals, in those days," Alex's mom says. "It's awful," she adds. "That's not the Olympic spirit. We're not just looking for medals. If you truly want medals, maybe you should only send those athletes who are ranked in the top three internationally."

"I contacted the COC many times and they stopped responding to my calls. I was fighting not only for Alex but for all the athletes."

The fight for the final spot in the Olympics was driving her crazy, she says. "I started keeping a journal that year, for my own sanity. It has been useful in many ways, including just keeping track of all the dates and competitions and awards. There has been so much to keep straight over the past decade."

Despite her best efforts, Marisa Orlando was not able

to move the COC, the FIG, or the IOC.

"I tried not to watch the 2004 Olympics on television," she says. "Alex watched, but she will watch any sporting event."

The Canadian Olympic Committee has changed their philosophy since the 2004 Olympic Games. "The COC doesn't have that silly rule any more about sending only the top 12 in the world to the Olympics," Marisa Orlando says.

"Erika-Leigh Stirton was in the same position at the same age. She qualified for the Olympics but missed the chance to go - twice. Erika and Alex talked and exchanged e-mails about all of that. It helped," she says.

"The biggest disappointment Alex had to face was not getting to go to the Olympics," her mother says. "Mixed in with that was her whole experience with Mary Sanders, who did get to go to the Olympics, by competing for the American team."

"Mary felt there was no other way to get into the Olympics, at that time, because of a new philosophy and plan put into practice by the Canadian Olympic Committee at that time. As everybody in Canada who follows the Olympics knows, the COC decided to support only those athletes who were ranked 12th or higher. To Mary, it seemed impossible to get to be 12th in the world in rhythmic gymnastics at that time, so she went to the Olympics with a country that did not have that philosophy."

"I wasn't happy she went, representing another country, but I was very happy she had the choice and that she was able to go to the Olympics. She did not train in the USA, she trained right here at Ritmika club. She only competed for the USA. It's quite complicated. We were very proud that Mary went to the Olympics, from our club, and we were very happy for her, but the fact that she was a Canadian who trained in Canada, right here at our club, did not get any attention during those Olympic Games."

Mimi Masleva was torn between two countries and it was a year of high stress for her when Alex and Mary were competing for Canada and the USA. "Mimi and I faced a lot of problems that year," Marisa Orlando says, "but I believe she always kept Alex's best interests in mind."

Alex still believes it was good for her to keep training with Mary.

"Mary wasn't supposed to train here," Marisa Orlando points out. "Alex and Mary were told that if they joined the American team, they would train at Lake Placid, in the USA. I didn't want Alex to miss school, so the Lake Placid plan didn't work for us. It never happened, though."

With the Olympic Games out of reach for the next four years, Orlando's future was uncertain.

"Alex had to decide what she wanted to do," her mother said, "this was a dream of hers since she was a very little girl and she worked very hard for her amazing ranking at world championships."

Alex did what she has always done after a disappointment. She trained harder, at a higher level, and kept on competing.

"I love the sport too much to just retire after one disappointment," Alex Orlando said. "I'd been looking forward to competing at the Commonwealth Games for years because we didn't get to compete in Manchester."

Gymnastics Canada, Ritmika Club, her family, her coach, and her mentors, including Lori Fung, all said they couldn't have been happier to see Alex rededicate her efforts. In addition to competing individually, they wanted her to assume a leadership role on a promising young Canadian national team.

"I thought she would quit after the big disappointment about the Olympics," her father says. "I told her that I was there to support her and she should follow her heart but I also told her not to quit on the emotion of the moment. You may regret it your whole life. But she made her own decision. It's just in her to do it, to train harder. It's not something I taught her. She has a goal in her mind and she's not going to be deterred."

Shortly after missing the Olympics, Alex returned to competition. She placed 15th All-around at the Deryugina Cup Grand Prix in Kiev, Ukraine. She competed at the Thiais Grand Prix in France, the Pacific Alliance Championships, the Baku Grand Prix in Azerbaijan, and the prestigious Corbeil-Essonnes Grand Prix in France.

At the Pacific Alliance Championships, Orlando was joined by Yana Tsikaridze, Pamela Jewell, and Stephanie Carew on the senior Canadian team. The junior team included Juliana Semenova, Katia Zaitseva, Suzy Lendvay, and Rosana Tso, the top four finishers at Elite Canada.

As a result of Canada's absence from the 2004 Olympic roster, the Pacific Alliance Championships served as the unofficial launch of the new generation of rhythmic gymnasts in Canada.

At the Olympic Games Alexandra missed, Russia finished 1st and 2nd in rhythmic. Three-time world All-around champ Kabaeva won gold. Mary Sanders was eliminated and FIG would not address concerns the Americans expressed over her scores.

The American gymnastics team protested the technical score of 4.600 out of 10.000 that Mary Sanders received in her hoop routine during individual All-around qualifications. Their claim stated that the score was unusually low, especially considering Sanders frequently scored much higher than that in national and world competitions. They also claimed that her Olympic hoop routine was free of visible or serious errors. The FIG, however, declined the protest, and additionally, never cited an explanation for the remarkably low score. Sanders received a 21.250 out of 30.000 in the hoop routine, leaving her to finish in 15th place out of 24, failing to qualify into the finals.

Even with her low score, which was disputed, Mary finished the qualifying round at the Olympics with a score of 90. Alex was considered very close to Mary, in terms of points scored, at that time. The athlete from Africa, who was given the final spot for rhythmic gymnastics at those Olympic Games, Wania Monteiro of Cape Verde, came last, with a score of 71.9.

The Women's Rhythmic Individual All-around winners were:

Alina Kabaeva, Russia - Gold

Irina Tchachina, Russia - Silver

Anna Bessonova, Ukraine - Bronze

"Missing Athens was really hard," Alexandra Orlando says. In the end, she had hoped to gain entry to that competition as one of two wild-card exemptions the rhythmic gymnastics federation permits. "I took some time off after just to think about everything because it was very difficult," Alexandra recalls. "I was only 17 at the time and felt I was getting better all the time. I loved the sport so I decided to keep on going as long as I enjoyed it as much as I did. I don't think you should retire after one bad competition or one bad experience."

Chapter 5. Best Friends, Biggest Competitors: The Alexandra And Mary Story

This is not the Nancy Kerrigan versus Tonya Harding opera but the friendship and rivalry between Alexandra Orlando and Mary Sanders would make a great movie, if only they weren't so nice and remained friends throughout the Olympic ordeal that put the two teammates who had been like sisters on competing teams for different countries. For a long difficult year it was Alexandra Orlando for Canada competing against Mary Sanders for the USA.

If only they had become bitter rivals and there was some physical violence, perhaps an unprovoked attack during the chaotic warm-ups before a major competition, caught by news cameras, with the American attacking the Canadian with rhythmic gymnastics clubs, or the Canadian going after the American with a rhythmic gymnastics rope, the sport and the athletes might have made the cover of *Time Magazine*, and others, making them more notorious, if not popular, that female hockey players in Canada and the USA.

In case the Kerrigan versus Harding controversy has faded from anyone's memory, here's a brief recap of what happened and how it all turned out.

Tonya Harding and Nancy Kerrigan

In the 1991 World Figure Skating Championships, Kerrigan received the bronze medal behind Kristi Yamaguchi and Tonya Harding. She received a bronze medal in the 1992

Winter Olympics, and the silver medal at the 1992 World Championships. The following season she became United States Champion and was leading the World Championship in Prague after the short program when a disastrous long program resulted in her tumbling to 5th in the standings and a win by Oksana Baiul.

Tonya Harding and Nancy Kerrigan were on the cover of TIME magazine in 1994 after Kerrigan was clubbed on the knee at a practice session during the 1994 US Figure Skating Championships. Harding became notorious for allegedly conspiring to harm Kerrigan. Harding admitted to helping cover up the attack. Harding's ex-husband accepted a plea bargain in exchange for his testimony against Harding. Harding avoided further prosecution and a possible jail sentence by pleading guilty to hindering the investigation of the attack and received three years probation, 500 hours of community service and a $160,000 fine. She maintains her innocence in the planning of the attack, contradicting the confessions of the alleged conspirators, and got a tattoo of an angel on her back, allegedly as a symbol of her innocence.

A short novel called <u>Celebrities In Disgrace</u>, by Elizabeth Searle, based on the so-called 'Kerrigan Attack', was adapted by Searle and composer Abigail Al-Doory to "Tonya And Nancy: The Opera," a chamber opera produced in 2006 by Tufts University and performed at the American Repertory Theatre's Zero Arrow Theatre in Cambridge, Massachusetts. The novella is also being adapted to a short film.

Tonya Harding went on to box on the Fox TV network Celebrity Boxing event. She made her official women's professional boxing debut, losing a four-round decision in the undercard of the Mike Tyson-Clifford Etienne bout, but Harding won her third pro fight. Harding was beaten in a match in Edmonton, Alberta by boxer Amy Paulson.

Somehow, Alexandra and Mary managed to make it through those Olympic years, remain friends, and avoid turning their relationship into some sort of soap opera.

"Mary and I were best friends from the time I was ten," Alex says. "She lived at my house for awhile and we started competing provincially together. She's two years older than me and was competing at a very high level so I learned a lot from her at that time. We accomplished a lot together. We were very strong together. Having the two of us on the same team meant we had a very strong team."

The Americans scouted both Mary and Alex and wanted them both for Team USA.

"We both have dual citizenship - Canadian and American - and we were both invited to go to the USA and compete for the American team," Alex says. "Mary decided to go and I decided to stay. Also, if I switched to the American team, I'd feel as though I was taking some other girl's spot. It happened to me. I went through the same sort of thing when I lost the wild card to Cape Verde. It's painful. It was a big decision, for me, and it would have had a big affect on the Canadian Rhythmic Gymnastics team. If Mary and I both left at the same time, Canada's top two competitors, the Canadian team would have dropped down quite a bit. We still trained together and worked out together."

"Mary and Alex were like the golden girls. They were like sisters," Marisa Orlando says. "Mary lived with us a few days a week when her family moved to Pickering, so that she could go to gym. I drove her everywhere. They really loved each other. Training together was great for both of them. Alex shows real fire out there, on the carpet. She has great passion and her spirit really shows. The Bulgarian style suits her and she suits it. Their movements flow with the music beautifully. Mary was more of technical performer. If you combined Mary and Alex, somehow, you would have the perfect athlete for rhythmic gymnastics. The combination would be unbeatable."

"I told Mary I didn't want her to go. Mary said, "I'll only go if Alex goes." But I talked her out of that. Financially, it was better for her. Ironically, right after she went, Alex started getting carding money in Canada."

Born in Oakville, Mary Sanders called Mississauga her hometown. She said her favourite song was "God must have spent a little more time on you", by NSYNC, and her favourite books were A Knight Without Armour, Jewel's book of poetry, followed by Way Of The Peaceful Warrior, by Dan Millman.

Mary tried artistic gymnastics before taking up rhythmic. She was coached by Bulgarian-born Mimi Masleva at Toronto's Ritmika club from the time she switched from artistic to rhythmic gymnastics. She won the Canadian National All-around title in 2001 and 2002. In late 2002 she decided to compete for the USA. In 2002 she swept the U.S. national championships, a feat she repeated in 2003 and 2004. Representing the US, Sanders has since placed 1st All-around at the 2003 Pan American Games and the 2004 Pacific Alliance Championships.

At World Championships in Budapest, Sanders finished 9th All-around in the qualifying competition, earning the United States a 2004 Olympic spot. She finished 10th in the All-around final - the best showing by an American in the competition's history. She also became the first American to make an individual event final, a feat she accomplished twice via her 7th place finish with hoop and clubs.

She said she was aiming for a top-eight finish at the Athens Games. The rhythmic competition started on her 19th birthday.

"Mary and Alex went to lots of competitions together with the same coach, representing Canada, and it was a little controversial to have the two of them competing for different countries, heading into the Olympics," says Annely Riga of Ritmika. "It was not easy. They had the same coach and I don't know how she did it, literally, because you cannot coach a girl competing for one country while you are dressed in the team uniform of another country."

Mary Sanders came 11th at the Varna World Cup, competing for the USA, and was officially declared Olympian when she won the USA Olympic trials.

Or, in the typically understated way the Americans have of describing things, Mary Sanders was the best rhythmic gymnast in the Western Hemisphere when she switched her competition flag to the Stars and Stripes. She sealed a US berth in the Olympics with her performance in the World Championships and she also won the Pan Am Games

Meanwhile, in Canada, at Nationals, Alexandra Orlando won five gold medals, was named National Champion and the #1 National Team Member.

What a year for Ritmika Centre for Gymnastics, with the top rhythmic gymnasts in Canada and the USA.

Mary Sanders was already a two-time Canadian National Champion in rhythmic gymnastics.

Her father, Fred, who was born in Michigan, had won the 1963 NCAA trampoline title. He introduced his daughter to gymnastics at age four. He died when Mary was just seven.

Mary's mother, Jaci, is Canadian-born, and had dual citizenship.

Mary was a member of the Canadian national team for five years but decided to compete for the USA to honour her father.

Changing allegiance was not an easy decision for her to make, she said at the time.

"I respected her decision and never gave her my opinion on the subject," Alex says. "A lot of factors influenced her. For instance, her mom was a single parent. My influences were different. My decision was based on the fact that I had an enormous amount of support here and because I had so many amazing experiences here."

The difficult situation had an unexpected benefit.

"While Mary was with the American team, the Canadian and American teams got along great," Alex says. "Mary and I wanted to hang out together, at competitions, and we were team leaders, so the rest of our teams all got along, became friends, and supported each other. Usually the Canadians and the Americans are very competitive, just like in women's hockey and other sports in which we both have good teams. The Canadians take a special kind of pride if we have a victory over the Americans."

"The English speaking countries came together when Mary and I were both competing. All the girls from Canada, the USA, England, and Australia bonded, for a while. But now a lot of those people have retired from the sport, so it's no longer the same."

"The girls on the Canadian team, for rhythmic gymnastics, are all great friends and very supportive of one another. We console each other. We have a lot of fun together, traveling the world. We have so many stories about flights and hotels we like to share and we get together to vent about coaches and talk about our amazing experiences in competitions."

"I travel alone a lot, so I value the time with the team even more."

Mary went into the worlds with a chance to better the best US finish ever, which was 24th by Jessica Howard in 1999. She finished 18th in the All-around as a member of the Canadian team in 2001, the year the USA did not compete in the championships because of the 9/11 terrorist attacks. At the 2003 World Championships, held in Budapest, Mary finished 8th in the preliminary round and 10th in the All-around final. She qualified for the finals in the hoop and the club. It was the first time the USA had an athlete qualify for finals in the World Championships in rhythmic gymnastics.

She won two US national championships and earned five gold medals at the Pan Am Games, competing for the USA.

Mary's Canadian training partner was named as her Athens alternate. If, for any reason, Mary Sanders was unable to go to the Olympics, Alexandra Orlando would go to Athens, instead. Mary said it was difficult and she did not talk about it a great deal with Alex but believed they were both there for each other no matter what happened. She also said she was trying to keep Alexandra motivated for the 2008 Olympics, in China.

"It was Alex who said "no" to the USA," her father says. "I told her it was her decision. I also told my wife, "Alex won't go". I knew what she would decide. I know my daughter is a true blue Canadian. She said, "No, I won't compete for the USA. What will I tell the little girls at the club?" She was worried more about the little ones who train at the same club as her in Canada. They respect her and look up to her. She was worried about what they would think if she switched allegiances to another country after competing for Canada for so long and growing up in Canada."

He believes she made the right decision. Although he is an American citizen and works in the USA, and the American team offered her money, better training facilities, and a better chance to get to the Olympics. "Yeah, it was the right decision for Alex," he says. "She feels strong about her heritage. She wouldn't have been happy wearing the uniform of any other country."

As for Mary, he says, "Mary wanted to get to the Olympics no matter what. Was it right or wrong, doing it the way she did? That's not for me to say. Only Mary can answer that. She's gotta live with that. Mary lived with us a couple of nights a week. She slept here, we fed her. My wife drove her everywhere. They were a team. She isn't mad about now but she was very surprised at the time. They could have been one helluva a team, Alex and Mary, if Mary stayed. It put Mimi in a difficult position, too. Coaching two girls competing against each other is hard. They were friends. They loved each other. How do you coach one girl to do better than the other girl and win for a different country and then coach the other girl to do better than her?"

"Anyway," he says, "the Olympics isn't about getting gold. It's about competing for your country. The Olympics is all about nationalism and how you feel about your country. When the flag of the country you are competing for is raised, you should feel something for that country. Athletes who compete for a different country can't feel the same way."

As it says in The Olympic Creed, "The most important thing in the Olympic Games is not to win but to take part, just as the most important thing in life is not the triumph but the struggle. The essential thing is not to have conquered but to have fought well."

"I got the feeling it wasn't meant for her, that year," Lori Fung says. "I talked to her during the time she was told she would be going and then wouldn't be going and she felt so disappointed. I told her to hang in there because it wasn't meant to be at that time. Maybe the next Olympics are the Games that are meant to be for Alex."

After the Olympics, Mary got into the University of Western Ontario but Cirque du Soleil contacted her and offered her an opportunity to perform with them and she signed their contract.

Before the Olympics, she was asked about her future plans and responded by saying she would probably go back to school, to a University in Canada, but she also said she wanted to go into something like Cirque du Soleil someday.

"I was very happy for Mary and the way things turned out for her with the Olympics," Marisa Orlando says. "She discussed the offer to join Cirque du Soleil with me, too. Her mom was worried that Mary would take that job and it would lead to many years of performing with them and Mary would never return to school."

"She discussed her decision with us and I encouraged her to go to school later," Annely Riga says. "I told her this was her opportunity of a lifetime and their first contract was for two years so she could do the other things she wants to do with her life after that. Mary really struggled, financially, as she had a single mother, who also had two boys to look after. I wanted Mary to succeed."

Mary Sanders retired from rhythmic gymnastics and she is now employed by Cirque du Soleil.

"I saw Mary in the show when Cirque du Soleil came to Toronto. She invited us backstage. It was great," Marisa Orlando says. "She has had some injuries, though, to her back and to her feet. She was planning to leave them, to go back to school, after just one year, instead of the two-year term they originally discussed."

Chapter 6. The Early Years Of Alex the Great

"I am a strong woman. I am a rhythmic gymnast. And, no, I wasn't born this way! It takes a LOT of work! And no, it's not easier than "regular gymnastics", ballet, track, etc. - combine all those and add the apparatus! All that and beauty and grace, too. On a regular basis, I overcome fear, pain, and my own limitations. Oh, and that new toss I've been working on? I caught it 150 times. I don't count the ones I don't catch."

~ anon

Are great athletes born or raised? Is it nature or nurture? Alex's mom says her second daughter was born with a lot of energy and a strong desire for attention and she turned that into a career as an elite athlete taking on the world in rhythmic gymnastics.

"She was born this way," her mother says. "She was very energetic from the start. When she started ballet, we saw she had more energy than anyone she danced with. Also, she always wanted attention. When she was a little kid in school, she was the student who always had her hand up to answer the teacher's questions. She had her hand up before the teacher asked questions. She would get very upset with herself if she wasn't at the top in school or ballet or whatever she did. She has always had a lot of determination. She always wants to look good, all the time, when she's competing."

"I wish I could take credit for it, but she was born with it," her father says. "She has my drive and ambition but it's unique, with her. She's very special. Right from the start, she had the talent and also the mindset. What she's doing, you don't learn. She sets goals and doesn't get swayed by anything along the way. And she truly loves her sport, rhythmic gymnastics. I had never heard of it until she started doing it."

Although he wanted his girls to take karate classes with him, he wanted them to find out what they liked and then do that. He had never heard of rhythmic gymnastics until his daughter got involved in it, but he learned to love the sport.

"Alex started ballet at six and she got into it, but then she discovered rhythmic gymnastics," he says. "I thought it was cute, in the beginning. Now I think it's a beautiful sport. I know how hard it is, how hard they train. And they make it look easy. I love the sport. It's beautiful."

"When I was a young man, I wanted a boy, because every guy thinks he wants that, but my wife's cousin had four girls, so I wasn't surprised we had two," her father says. "I'm Sicilian, and Alex takes after me. Some say she looks Spanish. Orlando is a Portuguese name. When she's in Puerto Rico, she looks Puerto Rican. When she was in Venezuela, she looked Venezuelan. When she goes to Brazil, she'll look Brazilian."

Alexandra was born on January 19, 1987, which makes her a Capricorn.

If she had a past life, it might have been as someone who was pushed around, put down, prevented from winning. In this life, Alexandra's karma is all about the pursuit of victory and winning. She started school in the Montessori system, tried the public school system for a while, and then attended a private girls school, which helped her focus on her training and competitions for her sport.

"I went to York Montessori School from K to Grade

Four," she says. "I still have some very good friends from those years."

Some of Alexandra's friends from her earliest days at school still keep track of her career and give her some support as fans. "I just got a card from them, signed by some of the teachers we had, including my Grade One teacher," she said.

"All the schools I went to helped. The co-ed public schools and the private all-girls school are quite different experiences."

"When Alex started competing, she did well at the provincial level, and she liked it," her mother remembers. "I wasn't interested in the competitions, at first; in fact, I thought the competitive stream was just a way for the club to make money. I never envisioned this! When Alex started rhythmic gymnastics as a little girl, I had no dream or plan to see her as a national champion competing for Canada at international events like the Commonwealth Games, the Pan Am Games, and the Olympics .... Alex was more of a natural than the girls she started rhythmic gymnastics with. Others had talent, too, but they disappeared a long the way, for different reasons. Alex always progressed. From the age of eight she has been very competitive in this sport. She has had amazing world-class coaches and that has helped enormously."

Another major influence in Alexandra's life, from the earliest years, was her sister, Victoria.

"Alex's sister was named after two grandfathers, both named Victor," the proud mother says. "I thought the name Alexandra went well with Victoria, so our two girls would be named Victoria and Alexandra."

Naming Victoria was easy," her father says. "She was our first, so we named her after my father, Victorio. My mother's father was named Victor. Naming our second daughter was not so easy. She's been pursuing victories since the day she was born. I'm the one who gave her the nickname, Alexandra The Great, but mostly we call her Alex."

He adds, "Also, I thought that being a woman with the name Alex might give her an advantage later in life. I can imagine her being in business, walking into a boardroom, introduced as Alex, and then everybody finds out she's a woman."

Being the big sister of a superstar is not an easy role to play.

"Her sister is proud of her," their mother says. "But it hasn't been easy for Victoria, having a younger sister who gets so much international attention. Most people think she's an only child or the oldest, if they know of Victoria."

The main difference between the two girls comes down to competition.

"Victoria is a wonderful soul," her mother says. "She does not have a competitive spirit at all. She did all the sports, growing up, and she was good, but she never liked the competitive part. The same is true for ballet and singing. She was a good ballerina and is a good singer, but she never wanted to compete with others to be the best at any of those things. She was always an excellent student, as well."

By the way, Alex also sings. "She has a very good voice," her mother says.

"I've had the Olympic dream since I was seven," Alex says. "I love competition. It makes some people so nervous they get sick, but it pumps me up. In Australia, I competed in front of crowds of ten thousand and I loved it."

"I started doing rhythmic gymnastics when I was five. I played soccer and basketball, too, and I did it all just for fun. At age seven, I started getting serious about rhythmic gymnastics because that's when I got into competitions and I discovered that I loved it. I dropped all the other sports I was interested in."

Alexandra's hero, on television, became a role model in real life.

"Back in 1996 I watched Camille Martens on TV," Alexandra says. "She was my hero and a great role model. When she was at the Olympics, my mom and I used to watch TV 24 hours a day to catch the moment she was on."

Her mom explains the real life connection.

"Evelyn Koop was the godmother of rhythmic gymnastics in Canada," she says. "She came to Canada from Estonia and she brought the sport with her. She used a movie studio in Toronto as a training facility. It was a good size, but that space made me nervous, at the time. My little girl disappeared into this big movie studio. Camille Martens trained with Evelyn Koop at that time, so Alex watched her train when she was on her way to the 1996 Olympics. Camille trained at her club, called Kalev Rhythmic Gymnastics Club, which was Alex's first club and where Alex was discovered."

"My mom has been the most involved in my athletic career," Alex says. "My dad has been my biggest fan. My sister, Victoria, is a terrific athlete, but she didn't like to compete. I love the competition. It's a bit of a mystery to me and to everyone why I've always loved that part of the sport. My dad also loves competition."

"Alex's dad is her biggest fan," her mother notes. "He raves about her."

"I played soccer for school teams until I was in Grade Seven," Alex recalls. "My big sister skated, so I tried figure skating, when I was young, and I liked it, but I loved rhythmic gymnastics, right from the start."

"Alex did not take figure skating, right away, but she loved skating," her mother says. "At skating practice, instead of doing figures, she used to race with a boy named Charlie, who became quite a good hockey player. They raced all the time and their way of stopping was to push each other into the boards and land on each other. Charlie stayed with hockey and became quite good. He played hockey for Upper Canada College, when he was in high school."

Alex now works out with some of Canada's Olympic figure skaters and hockey players at a club in Toronto.

"When she was little, Alex had a bowl cut, or a mushroom cut," her mother recalls.

"She was a tomboy and she liked having short hair," her mother recalls. "When she first went to competitions for rhythmic gymnastics, everybody looked at her funny and convinced her she should have long hair. That was hard for her, at the time."

"I remember her at age nine with that short, boyish, haircut and her plain leotards, going to the provincial championships. She didn't look like the other girls but the way she competed was amazing," her father says. "I loved watching her."

Alex's second sport, after rhythmic gymnastics, is not skating, it's soccer.

"Alex played soccer as a little girl and she still wants to play," her mother says. "I wouldn't be surprised if she started playing soccer after she retires from rhythmic gymnastics."

Although she was something of a tomboy and obviously a gifted athlete, at a young age, Alexandra also liked to act like a "girly girl", to use her expression, too.

"Alex is an amazing athlete. She was great at soccer and when she tried track events, but she loves to get dressed up and put on make-up, too," her mother says. "She really likes it, but she doesn't get to do it very often. Maybe that's why she likes it so much."

Her parents believe she takes after her father more than her mother.

"I was a girly girl, not an athlete," her mother says. "I didn't do any sports. In school, I was the last one picked for teams. Alex takes after her dad more than her mom."

Because of her dad's influence, Alex might have studied karate instead of rhythmic gymnastics.

"Her dad played sports, especially baseball, and still does martial arts. He has a black belt in karate and had both our girls taking karate for a while," his wife explains. "His sensei wanted to work with Alex as soon as he saw her as he recognized her talent in this area."

Alex's parents have given her incredible support even though they did not experience the same sort of parental backing when they were kids.

"If her dad had the opportunities to pursue sports, he might have gone somewhere with baseball," she says. "He is always saying, 'Nobody ever watched me play baseball'." We give Alex so much support and attention, going to so many competitions, and he always says, "I never got this kind of support."

"I wanted a dad like me," he says. "My dad was great, but he didn't have time to come to my little league games or baseball games in high school. In that generation, they didn't travel around like we do, following their kids. I wanted to do better than my father. My dad wanted to drop me off and then leave. He had other things he had to do. Sometimes he didn't even drop me off. He worked hard, for the post office, as a dispatch manager."

Paul Orlando supports Alex in every way he can.

"I'm her biggest fan but I'm not always there to watch her train, all those hours, every week," her father says. "I can't go to all the meets. You can't go to them all."

"I was at Melbourne to see her triumph and I'll be going to China, too," her mother says.

"We spent a fortune on this sport," she adds. "We had no family vacations for years and no furniture in our house. My friends all said, "You must be crazy". Nobody pays for training camps so we have to cover that. There are very good camps in Bulgaria, Russia, and France."

When it came down to making a choice of being a coach or a mom, Marisa Orlando always chose the role of the mom. Sometimes she had to coach her daughter on how to work with her rhythmic gymnastics coach.

"When Alexandra was age eight, Ritmika, her club, asked me if I wanted to help. I said, 'Yes', and they never let go!" Marisa Orlando says. "I'm not complaining. I learned a lot and I stayed in my daughter's life. I learned how to put on a world-class competition. I was on the board of the Ontario Gymnastics Federation for four years and also helped out with Gymnastics Canada during competitions. I was Alex's driver, worked on her competition suits, spent hours and hours listening to music with her, to choose the right pieces for competition. I was also there where she cried."

It is hard to imagine Alex the Great crying but imagine the national champion as a young girl.

"Sometimes I was like a coach, but not when she cried," her mom says. "Some moms act hard, like a coach, all the time. But whenever Alex cried, I stopped being a coach and was a mom, again. I'm her shoulder; that's my main job. When Alex needs a shoulder to cry on, it's her mom's shoulder."

"Alex didn't get much sympathy from me when she complained about the repetition, the need to do the same thing over and over, or the coach's insistence that she repeat something long after she felt she no longer needed to," her mother says. "That was her main complaint - the repetition."

In a sport that is won or lost by fractions or decimals, and judged on so many technical and artistic points, coaches believe the best way to prepare for competition is through repetition. They watch the same athlete perform the same routine hundreds of times, watching every movement, isolating each body part, analyzing the use of the apparatus, contemplating the costume and make-up, listening to the music and watching how well the athlete's movements flow on the carpet.

"Alex phoned, sometimes, from training, and I would coach her to get right back in there and keep trying," her mother recalls. "That's the hardest thing for a parent to do. You want to give your kid a hug, take your daughter home. But that's not always the best thing to do and it's not always possible, particularly if your kid is training somewhere faraway like Bulgaria or Japan."

Alex did, in fact, phone home in tears, one time, while training in Japan.

"When Alex called from Japan, crying, saying she was thinking about quitting, I didn't know what to tell her," her mother recalls. "That was in 2003, in that same era of the Olympic disappointment. She cried when she had big disappointments. When she got the news about the last Olympics, she cried. She deserved to go to those Olympics. She earned it. She was told she would be going. And then she was told she couldn't go. She cried over that. However, when she came home, she snapped out of it, decided to stick with it, trained harder and harder, at higher levels of difficulty, and found even more success."

Alexandra's mother says she had to learn a lot, as the mother of an elite athlete, and it was all new to her. "I wasn't brought up that way," she says. "I was never pushed to work that hard."

She is quick to add, "The coaches are strict and there is a lot of discipline. Alex's first coach, at Kalev, was Russian and she had a very technical approach. Her first coach, Svetlana, had a great deal to do with Alex's early success. This was at Kalev club. Mimi isn't the kind of coach who calls you on every little thing. She came here from Japan, after Bulgaria, and was used to working with girls who were far removed from their parents."

When Marisa Orlando needed help, when it came to coaching her daughter on how to work with her coach, she went straight to the top, calling on Canada's rhythmic gymnastics Olympic gold medallist.

"Lori Fung helped with that a great deal by telling Alex, 'The coach is pushing you because she believes in you. It's a good thing that she believes you can perform at such a high level.' Alex understood after a while, but it's hard for a little girl."

Marisa Orlando has the highest praise for Lori Fung.

"She was an amazing athlete, winning Olympic gold in 1984, in Los Angeles," she says. "Lori Fung has also been great with Alex. She says she would do anything for Alex and was a huge help during the Olympics disappointment."

"I have a great deal of respect for my coach," Alex says. "True, it was hard for me to understand her, at the beginning. Now my coach and I have a great understanding. If she got upset with me in the gym, I learned how to take it. It was a challenge, at the time, but afterwards, I was very grateful.

After going through all that, you can love your coach more."

Although Alex experienced occasional frustrations, working with her coach, she did not show a great deal of sympathy when someone older at the club was having a hard time and hearing about it from a coach. Alex's competitive side came out, instead. If someone younger was having problems, she would try to help them out.

Ritmika's president also helped out if there was a conflict between a young athlete and her coach.

"I think there are two kinds of people in the world: Those who complain, and those who do things," she says. "When we get complainers in our club, I tell them they have to make a choice. We have lots of pep talks."

Alex was far less likely to get upset with her coach during training than she was to get upset with herself after a competition.

"If Alex is going to get upset, it won't be before a competition. Sometimes she freaks out after a competition," her mother says. "She has little fits of craziness but I can always calm her down."

"She never liked the repetitive part of training," her father says. "It was the same in martial arts. You have to do it a million times, and then you finally get it. Alex always got it very fast and felt she didn't have to do it a million more times. But that's how you coach these sports. It's up to the coach. It's all in the way you approach an individual, get them motivated. Training can be monotonous. A lot depends on the coach's personality. But Alex is a pro. She knows what she's doing when she's training. She never liked repeating something after she felt she had it."

Alex admits to 'freaking out' when she was a much younger competitor.

"The disappointments are harder on the younger competitors," she says. "I never freak out, any more; I just use the experience to become even more determined to show the judges the next time."

That's how a champion handles that sort of stress. It is one of Alex's secrets of success.

"Now that I'm older, I know you can learn a lot from that kind of disappointment," she says. "The trick is to avoid feeling singled out. I go back to training and increase the level of difficulty and work harder so I'll perform even better the next time."

"After five weeks of training in Bulgaria, I hardly recognized my own daughter. She walked into the competition with so much confidence and such a great sense of calm. It was really something", Marisa Orlando says.

At age ten, Alex started competing at the national level.

In 1997, she was 6th overall at Elite Ontario, 4th overall at Eastern Regionals, and 4th overall at the National Championships.

The next year, she was 2nd overall and 1st in Rope at the Questo Invitational; 3rd overall with a 1st in Ball, 2nd in Hoop, and 3rd in Rope at Elite Ontario; 2nd overall at the Eastern Regionals; and 3rd overall, with a 1st in Hoop and 2nd in Rope at the National Championships.

At age 13, Alexandra was the Novice Ontario Champion at the Elite Ontario Championships and the Novice National Champion at Montreal Nationals.

At 14, she became Junior National Champion.

She was also 1st All-around at Elite Ontario, 1st All-around at Portugal Invitational, with four gold medals in finals, and 1st All-around at National Championships in

Edmonton, with four gold medals in finals.

She took 4th place at an international competition in Bulgaria that year, as well.

Chapter 7. Under The Influence:
Mimi Masleva, Annely Riga, Lori Fung,
Camille Martens, Maria Petrova,
Erika-Leigh Stirton, The Family, and Canada

(When asked if she felt like she wanted to give up in train-ing) "Yes, very often! But at the same time I realize that I can't live without rhythmic gymnastics. It's the most important thing in my life."

~ Ekaterina Serebrianskaya,
International Gymnast Magazine

"When Alex won her second seniors national champi-onship - she was novice champion, then junior champion, and then seniors champion for two years in a row - I realized she was headed for the very top," her father says. "Also, I knew how hard she trained."

Alexandra competed internationally for half a decade before her mother was convinced she was headed for the top, in her sport.

"The first time I had a strong sense that she was head-ed for the very top was when she was 12-years-old and she went to Europe. Mary Sanders went with her. Alex was a novice in Canada, but she was allowed to compete as a junior in Europe. The coaches put together the choreography Alex needed to compete. In a competition in France, on the first day, Alex came out ahead of Mary."

It wasn't just winning that impressed Alexandra's

mother, it was the way she performed and won.

"The way she did it amazed me. That was the first time she performed in front of a huge crowd. In Canada, there would be two or three people in the audience, but in Europe there are big crowds with thousands of people. Whole families go to watch the competitions together and the crowd makes a lot of noise, cheering on the gymnasts. Compared to that, it is like a morgue at competitions here. If someone drops a club or a ball, here, the people in the audience gasp, as though something horrible has happened. In Europe, they cheer on the person who dropped the club or the ball, because they want them to do well."

Another defining moment for the mother of the athlete came in the jungles of Venezuela.

"When we went to the Junior Pan Am Games, in Venezuela, we discovered their government had built a great facility three hours outside the city, surrounded by jungle. In that unlikely location, they had a huge sculpture outside the building and it was a rhythmic gymnast. We couldn't believe it; we thought it was fantastic."

The venue in Venezuela was unlike competition locations in Canada for another reason, as well.

"The sports facility was in a compound and we couldn't leave. Also, there were signs saying 'No Guns'."

The stands filled up and the noise was tremendous.

How did the young Alex perform in this environment?

"Alex had a lot of competition from the South American girls on their home turf, but Alex came out on top and was the Junior Pan Am champ," her mom reports.

"In 2003 we went to Budapest and it was beautiful to see rhythmic gymnastics in a place like that. Alex loved it. The stadium was packed, with 40,000 people, for "the worlds", watching the top girls from all over the world."

How did Alex climb to these heights, starting at such a young age?

Alexandra Orlando's major influences include her parents, her sister, her coach, her club, her country, and some of the major figures in rhythmic gymnastics in Canada and the world, especially Maria Petrova, the champion rhythmic gymnast from Bulgaria who has helped her with choreography, Lori Fung, the first Olympic gold medal winner in rhythmic gymnastics, Camille Martens, who she watched train for the Olympics, and Erika-Leigh Stirton, who had great success at the Commonwealth Games before her.

The Dimitritchka "Mimi" Masleva Story

Dimitritchka Masleva, better known as "Mimi", is an internationally-renowned rhythmic gymnastics coach who started her career in Bulgaria and then coached in Japan before moving to Canada, and who has been involved in rhythmic gymnastics for over two decades.

She is a coach who has guided the development of world champions in many countries, including the USA and China, as well as Canada, Japan, and Bulgaria.

She earned a degree from the Higher Institute of Physical Culture in Sofia, Bulgaria in 1979, has been honoured as a Master of Sports and a Distinguished Coach by the Bulgarian Government, and was the national coach of the award-winning Bulgarian Group Team from 1985 to 1989. Under Mimi, the Bulgarian Group Team won the European Champion title three times, became World Champions twice, and also won the World Cup.

In 1989, Mimi was relocated to Japan, by the government of Bulgaria, and became the head coach of the Jusco RSG Club. Every year for five years, from 1992 to 1996 the Jusco team was the champion in the Japanese competitions. One of her gymnasts, Yamada Miho competed in the 1996 Atlanta Olympic Games.

During her time in Japan, Mimi was invited to Beijing to train the Chinese National Team. The following year, the Chinese gymnasts won seven gold medals in the Four Continents Competition in Egypt. The Chinese Group Team also participated in the 1996 Atlanta Olympic Games and placed fifth.

Mimi grew up in Bulgaria when it was under communism. She reports that the Soviet system of government treated its elite athletes very well. "We were treated like golden girls," she recalls. "In the Communist era, coaches were free to do whatever they wanted with their athletes, and they completely controlled them. That led to some problems. It also led to the development of many great athletes. In order to compete for the Soviet Union at the Olympics, you had to compete with elite athletes from all the Soviet countries first."

After arriving in Canada, she coached both Alexandra Orlando and Mary Sanders for many years at Ritmika, taking them to international events to compete for Canada, and later found herself in the awkward position of coaching for two countries at the same time. She coached Mary Sanders at international competitions for the American team and, at the same time, coached Alex Orlando, who competed for Canada.

She now works at Seneca College as well as Ritmika Gymnastics Centre and coaches only for Canada but maintains strong connections with the rest of the rhythmic gymnastics world, particularly in Bulgaria, Japan, and China. She is working primarily with Ritmika's national competitors, and coaching Alexandra one-on-one as much as possible.

In Canada, she says, there should be more support for rhythmic gymnastics from the government and from people across the country. "The winter sports are strong in Canada and get a lot of support, especially hockey," she notes. "The Winter Olympics will be in Canada in 2010. There is nothing wrong with the focus on hockey in Canada, but there are other sports to focus on, too. For girls, especially, in addition to hockey, there should be a strong national program for rhythmic gymnastics. We should give other sports room to grow."

The Annely Riga Story

Annely Riga, president of Ritmika Rhythmic Gymnastics Club, the club where Alexandra has trained for many years, has many memories of the young Alex.

"Alexandra was a little star ever since she was a little girl," she says.

"Right from the start, she had it inside of her," she explains. "She has that spark and also the ability to project it. Those are the two greatest things that are the secrets to her success."

Alexandra's secret of success?

"She trains hard, has had good coaching and the support of her family, as well as our club, but that spark she has inside of her, the ability to project it, and her passion for her sport are the keys to her success."

There is much more to rhythmic gymnastics than athleticism, she says.

"Rhythmic gymnastics is not only a sport," she explains, "it's also art and performance. The athletes give artistic performances that express the feelings they have inside. Alex is a great athlete, artist, and performer, with a gift for expressing that spark she has inside. You have to be passionate about it"

The odds were stacked against Alexandra, despite her gifts and talents, Riga says. "She is the only person in her family and in her extended family who competes in this or any sport at such a high level. Alex's sister is also very athletic and talented but she does not like to compete. Alex loves to compete."

She gives some credit to the club and Alex's coaching but gives most of the credit to Alexandra, herself.

"That's the sign of a champion," she says. "We have many girls at our club and they have had excellent coaching; we have had a number of national champions. But it's mostly her," Riga says, "and it's all about her spark, her commitment, her passion, and her ability to express herself on the carpet as an athlete, artist, and performer."

On the other hand, Alex's family has been very supportive. "Her whole family is behind her," Riga says. "It has been very expensive, traveling around the world to competitions. Her family has donated an enormous amount of time doing everything from driving Alex to the club for coaching, training, and competitions, to getting involved in fundraising. Her mom has driven her everywhere, all these years, and her mom has also done fundraising and got involved with the sport."

As for Ritmika, her club, she says, "I didn't know how to stop. I didn't have good financial advice or assistance."

"I was born into rhythmic gymnastics in Estonia. Rhythmic gymnastics was my training and education was all about it. I was a gymnast there. I trained and competed and then coached at the University level, as well as in sports schools. When I got married and emigrated, I thought I would be a housewife in Canada, but I discovered I could not just sit at home. I found an Estonian gymnastics club and coached there for two years. I wound up coaching 99% of their classes so I thought about starting my own club. With another coach as a partner, I set up Ritmika 26 years ago. We had 300 gymnasts our first year and used to rent school gyms, churches, halls. It was 14 years of pure hell, running around getting permits and going to different locations all the time. We did not start the competitive stream for five years."

"Those places had low ceilings and no carpets. The girls did okay but we wanted a better place for them. We were not ambitious, in the beginning, but we saw some nice talent and we did not want to lose those girls to competitive clubs. I was greedy, I guess, because I wanted to keep those talented girls, and so we started to offer a competitive stream in rhythmic gymnastics at our club."

"First, I had to look for a facility. It had to be a place with very high ceiling. Just when I thought I had found one, my partner retired. So, I did it solo. That led to ten years of struggle. The space was too expensive. Even so, we got great results, starting in the very first year. Before long, we had national champions."

"We had the coaches and the competitors but it was a struggle financially so I sold that place and looked for a new location. Our current location is much better, beside a new mall and housing developments. It is clean and beautiful. We are happy here."

"There is no dance studio here, yet, but we hope one gets built on top of our gymnastics space. We are leasing this space but the owner is open to building the dance studio. We had a ballet teacher from Bulgaria. Alex started ballet with our club, too. Our dance teacher worked with Alex's coach in

Japan. I saw them there and brought them to Canada."

"I don't want to brag," Annely Riga says. "I never do. But Ritmika has promoted the sport in Canada very well. We have no national sports centre for this sport. I have kept the club going and it has promoted the sport in Canada. Three out of the eight girls on Canada's national team are from our club."

"Alex is the current Canadian champion. Mary was Canadian champion before her. We've had the Canadian champion eight times."

"The 2nd ranked rhythmic gymnast in Canada is also a member of our club. Carly Orava is 17 and she did well at the 2006 Commonwealth Games, as did Natalie Ngo, who is ranked 8th in Canada. She is 16-years-old."

"There's one girl coming up who is like a little Alex, with that spark in her eyes, and a few others who may be good, like her, and compete internationally."

"This sport also teaches discipline. All the girls who do well here do well in school, too, because they have the discipline and they learn a lot about time management. People who can schedule their time and do many things at the same time find a lot of success in life. Look at all the people who volunteer in this country and what they manage to do."

"It takes years to become a champion and it depends on the girl, her schooling, her family, funding. Alex now has some funding from Sports Canada, finally. When one of our athletes competes, we have to send the athlete, her coach, and a judge, and it's very expensive."

"I had to sell my house because of this sport. I bought the old gym, which was the home of our club. We had athletes who had to go on and compete, I believed, so I kept supporting them."

"In the days of Lori Fung, when the Olympics were

held in Los Angeles, we were first and won the gold medal, the year the Soviet Union boycotted the games. We had lots of funding in that era and it was great. When the funding went down, all the way to zero, Canada's results went down, too."

"We went to competitions using our own money, covering training, athletes, judges, coaches, travel and accommodations. The people from other countries could not believe it."

"This year, Alex will work with Mimi one-on-one, at Ritmika, much of the time. Of course, Mimi also works at Seneca and she coaches lots of girls at Ritmika. We're looking for a better facility for training so Mimi can work with Alex one-on-one in a place where there is enough room for a high ceiling and a big carpet. Etobicoke has the best facility in the country. The problem is that nobody in Canada has a permanent facility for this sport."

The Lori Fung Story

In 1976, 13-year-old Lori Fung started training in rhythmic gymnastics. It turned out to be the perfect fit. She competed in her first National Championships just a year after taking up the sport. She went on to become the world's first rhythmic gymnastics Olympic Champion.

Born February 21, 1963, in Vancouver, British Columbia, she studied under many coaches, but the biggest influence came from the great Bulgarian coach Liliana Dmitrova. In 1981, she represented Canada at her first World Championships. She placed 30th and that was considered a real accomplishment in a field of Eastern-bloc athletes.

After winning the Canadian Nationals in 1982, she triumphed at the Four Continents Championships.

In 1983, she again won Canadian Nationals, and also took gold at the Swiss Invitational. She moved up to 23rd All-around at the World Championships. That result, and the knowledge that rhythmic gymnastics would be included in the next Olympics, inspired her. She finished high school by correspondence so she could train even more seriously.

Prior to the Olympics, Fung placed 12th at the Poznan Invitational and 18th at both Corbeil and the Brother Cup.

The Eastern-bloc countries boycotted the Olympics in L.A. in 1984 but, Fung still had to defeat the strong Romanian and West German contingents. One of Lori's best friends was Lilia Ignatova from Bulgaria who was ranked number one going into the Olympics. With the boycott, Lilia was not able to attend and she and Lori cried together in Japan at the Brother Cup. Lilia gave Lori a four-leaf clover that Neshka Robeva had given her to win the Olympics. Lilia asked Lori to go to Los Angeles and win for her. "Deep down in my heart, I know that Lilia was there with me in Los Angeles. Maybe that was the little extra I needed to win."

At the Olympic Games, Lori's precise technique, choreography, and enthusiastic presentation captivated the audience and the judges. While performing at the highest level of difficulty, she kept a cheerful expression on her face. Everyone who saw her was convinced she put her heart and soul into her routines and it never failed to rouse crowd support.

The new Olympic champion was a celebrity in Canada and around the world. She was invited to perform for VIPs, such as Pope John Paul II, Prince Charles and Princess Diana, Elton John, and the Prime Minister of Canada.

Shortly after her Olympic victory, Lori won her 2nd Four Continents title. She continued training, and placed 9th at the 1985 World Championships. It should be noted that the World Championships were attended by the countries that did not go to the Olympics the year before.

In 1987, while traveling to the World Championships, she had an attack of appendicitis, was rushed to the hospital, and was forced to sit out the competition.

After retiring in 1988 as the Olympic gold medal winner, seven-time Canadian National Champion, and four-time Four Continents Champion, she was inducted into the British Columbia Hall of Fame, the Canadian Hall of Fame, and the FIG Hall of Fame. She was also given the Order of British Columbia and the Order of Canada.

Since retiring as a competitive athlete, she has became a judge for rhythmic gymnastics, served as a coach for the American, Mexican, and Canadian National Teams. She is currently a consultant of Club Elite Rhythmics in Vancouver, which was the club she founded. Lori Fung has been the honourary Chairperson of the Canadian Cancer Society and has appeared on TV, radio, and in-person to promote fitness in Canada. She is also an active motivational speaker.

The Camille Martens Story

Camille Martens, the Canadian gymnast, was best known for her smooth, mature style and ability to express her love of performance in every routine. "The little Alex used to watch Camille Martens train for the Olympics at the Kalev club and that had a huge influence on her, as a little girl," her mother recalls.

"The level of training was impressive," she says. "Alex found it a little scary that Camille Martins' coach made her do the same thing 100 times, until she got it right. That was what irritated Alex most, in her own training; she was always wondering why she had to do the same thing over and over again when she felt she "had it"."

The history of this sport in Canada is not long and

deep, as in some European countries, but is developing depth and Alexandra Orlando is the direct heir of a dynasty that includes other Canadian champions and some of them have won gold medals at the Olympics. Alexandra Orlando grew up watching Camille Martens and Camille Martens grew up watching Lori Fung. Alexandra has benefited enormously from the example and the influence of both of these Canadian rhythmic gymnastic superstars.

When Camille Martens was just an eight-year-old girl, she watched the 1984 Olympics on television, along with millions of other sports fans. Unlike most other people watching the Olympics on TV that year, she knew immediately she wanted to be a rhythmic gymnast.

She says the beauty, grace, and skills were irresistible to her. She told her father that she would someday be in the Olympics and she sounded quite confident about it, for an eight-year-old.

Little did her father know that the child's prophecy would come true.

Two years later, Martens met Lori Fung. Camille Martens began taking her training completely seriously right after meeting the first Olympic Champion in rhythmic gymnastics.

At age 11, Martens moved away from home to train. Within a few years, the sacrifices she made paid off: Camille Martens became the Canadian Junior Champion at age 14.

She won her first Senior National title a couple of years later and then headed to the World Championships.

In 1993, Martens placed a respectable 21st in the All-around at "The Worlds".

The following year, she took home more medals than any other Canadian gymnast at those Commonwealth Games:

six medals including gold for team, silver for the All-around, and silver for each event final.

She also picked up a bronze in the All-around at the Four Continents Championships that year.

She changed coaches after the next World Championships, going with the Bulgarian coach Ludmilla Dimitrova. Under Dimitrova's guidance, she came 11th at the Kalamata Cup, 6th at the Shishmanova Cup, and 14th at Corbeil.

Martens' international accomplishments earned her Canada's a spot in the 1996 Olympics.

After her Olympic goal was met, she retired, got married, and started her own rhythmic club, Okanogan Rhythmics, in her hometown of Vernon, BC.

In 1999 she returned to competition and placed 5th All-around at the 1999 Canadian National Championships.

That was the year Alexandra Orlando came into prominence. At age 12, she watched Martens and then she swept the All-around and individual title in the novice competition of the 1999 Canadian Championships.

"Camille Martens was training when my sister was at the Kalev RG club," Victoria Orlando recalls. "Camille was friendly with all the girls and when I went to the shows she'd always talk to me. I always liked her and I was also in awe of her. She was such a powerful gymnast, she made you want to watch her. She was tall and beautiful, not a stick, like some athletes. She was a beautiful athlete. My sister is like that, too. They are strong Canadian women. The toothpick girls don't have the strength and the passion you see when they perform."

"Some gymnasts are not nice," Victoria adds, "particularly those who get to a higher level. It goes to their heads.

Some of them just don't know how to deal with the success and the attention. Others deal with it with grace and modesty. That's what Camille was like, even when she came back from Olympics. She said she was just happy she got the chance to go."

The Maria Petrova Story

"But one thing's for sure, I won't give up gymnastics. It's cool."

~Maria Petrova

Maria Petrova, who had a long reign on top of the rhythmic gymnastics world, was born in Bulgaria on November 13, 1975. She has won more European titles than anyone. She is regarded as one of the finest rhythmic gymnasts of all time, and never placed lower than 7th in any competition in her entire career. She also had two more world titles. Although she tried to retire several times after her first World title, Petrova hung on as a favor to the Bulgarian national team, which was in a rebuilding phase after the collapse of communism in the Eastern European countries.

Despite a clean, mature, expressive performance - that included a wonderfully modern rope exercise, an almost perfectly executed ball routine, and sophisticated Spanish-style clubs and ribbon that bettered the majority of the top performers, at the 1996 Olympics Petrova wound up in the exact spot (5th) that she had finished in the Olympics four years earlier. Some cited Petrova's lack of difficulty as the reason for her off-the-podium placement, but far more rhythmic fans, and even Petrova herself, were convinced Petrova was finally able to retire after her Olympic disappointment, turning full-time to her studies at the Bulgarian National Sports Academy.

Petrova was born and grew up under communism, when Bulgaria was a country completely dominated by the Soviet Union. A native of Plovdiv, Bulgaria, Petrova began training at the age of five at the Levski club under the guidance of Natalia Muravenova.

In her first World Championships in 1991, she narrowly missed making the All-around final after an untimely hoop drop. Nevertheless, she made quite an impression, causing judges and journalists alike to buzz about this amazing new talent. At the 1992 European Championships, Petrova scored her first major victory.

Expectations were high at the Barcelona Olympics, but Petrova found herself in 5th place after a penalty of 0.20 was assessed because the zipper on the back of her leotard broke during her hoop exercise. At the World Championships just a few months later, Petrova took 2nd behind Oksana Kostina and ahead of Larissa Lukyanenko.

In 1993, Petrova went to Worlds armed with one of the best sets of routines ever performed. She also competed a fast, folksy exercise with ribbon, and a funky, small-toss-filled clubs routine to Suzanne Vega's "Tom's Diner." But it was her intense interpretation of Carmina Burana that caused the crowd to erupt into resounding ovation. She won the All-around, as well as three more gold medals (ball, hoop, ribbon) and a bronze clubs.

In 1998, she married long-time boyfriend Borislav Mihailov, the decorated former goalkeeper of the Bulgarian national soccer team. Petrova has been elected to the Administrative Council of the Bulgarian Rhythmic Gymnastics Federation, and she hoped to become a judge when she has completed her University studies.

A French perfume company released a new fragrance

called Maria P., and its ads feature glamorous shots of the former gymnast.

"Maria Petrova, the great rhythmic gymnast from Bulgaria, is going to help Alex with choreography," Marisa Orlando says. "Maria loves Alex, the way she approaches the sport and competes, and the judges in Europe have compared Alex's style to Maria's, which is a great compliment."

The Erika-Leigh Stirton Story

"Rhythmic gymnastics has been my life and my world. Gymnastics has made me who I am. It has shaped my character, developed me mentally and emotionally and helped prepare me to be successful in the future. I have had so many wonderful times and met so many fabulous people and I know the memories I have will last long after the medals are tarnished and the scores forgotten. This year was one of my greatest achievements because I learned to compete for me, and for the joy and love I have for rhythmic gymnastics and not for the outcome. I truly realized why I was in this sport and why I continued in it for so long. Success is achieved along the way, and I truly believe that it is the journey that is important - not the destination. I am frightened at the direction that rhythmics is headed in. From my perception it is becoming too political, too unethical and too corrupt at an alarming rate. I do not know how we can improve the situation, but I am happy that I will no longer be in a position where my performance will not be judged by what I do on the floor. I am going to miss the sport tremendously but I am looking forward to pursuing new aspects of life. The greatest quote I have heard is this: "A real champion is a champion in life, not just in sport."

~Erika-Leigh Stirton, from her retirement speech

The 1997 and 1998 Canadian senior rhythmic gymnastics champion was destined to be a strong contender at the 2000 Olympics in Sydney, but something happened, as they say.

Erika won five gold medals at the 1998 Commonwealth Games. She was 2nd team, 1st All-around and 1st in all four apparatus at the Aeon Cup in Tokyo. At the 1997 World Championship in Berlin, she qualified 7th and finished 20th overall. At the 1995 World Championships, she was 24th, and at the 1994 Junior Pan Am Cup in Mexico, she was #1. She was also the Canadian Junior Champion.

Erika was born in 1980, in Oakville, grew up in Mississauga, and trained with at the Etobicoke Olympium RSG Club, and became known as the Canadian rhythmic gymnastic champion who roped in five gold medals at the Commonwealth Games in Kuala Lumpur.

She proved herself the Commonwealth's undisputed queen of rhythmic gymnastics in 1998 with a clean sweep of gold medals by following up her win in the All-round competition by adding the individual rope, hoop, clubs and ribbon titles. She scored more than 9.5 in each routine, with 9.650 in the ribbon, her best, to match the five gold medals of Kasumi Takahashi, the Australian champion.

The Marisa Orlando Story

Alexandra's mother has taken on many roles in support of her daughter's career as an athlete, including the role of coach, to some degree.

She points out that she did not expect, anticipate, or plan for her daughter to be an elite athlete. It came as a complete surprise.

"My plan, after my daughters were born, was to go back to work, after a couple of years," Marisa Orlando says. "I had worked at a brokerage on Wall Street. I took a two-year break but it never ended."

Once Alexandra got involved in competitive rhythmic gymnastics, her mother's life took a new direction.

"I was not a stockbroker, but over the past decade I helped my husband with his business and projects, but this sport demanded so much attention," she says. "I don't regret it. It has been quite a ride. I had no sports background, so entering into the world of sports was really something. I got to see so much of Canada and the world, even the jungles of Venezuela .... "I've met so many lovely families all across Canada and in Europe through this sport. I became the mom with the video camera at so many competitions. I have so much footage. Before I show it to anyone, I'll have to get someone to edit out me screaming."

"When Alex was younger, I went to quite a few competitions overseas but now I stick to Canada."

"Our family is in New York and in Italy. Rhythmic gymnastics is huge in Italy but Alex has never competed there. The timing has never been ideal. Whenever there was a competition in Italy where our friends and family could have seen Alex perform, there was a more important event being held somewhere else."

Her mother has continued to be Alex's main supporter and her father is still her number one fan.

"Both my parents have done an enormous amount for me," Alex notes. "My mom has been my manager and agent, on top of everything else. We talked about getting an agent to represent me. So far, my mom has been my agent and manager. She's great at it. Everything goes through my mom. If you want to get to me, you have to go through my mom."

Not just any mom can take on the role of manager and

agent for an elite athlete in world competition.

"She says it feels weird, sometimes, to promote your daughter the way an agent does," Alex says, "but she has experience working with Gymnastics Canada and Gymnastics Ontario, so she knows what she's doing."

"I've been looking for an agent, but it isn't easy. So far, I'm Alex's agent, her manager, and her mom, but there are some things I cannot do."

The Paul Orlando Story

Alexandra's father, Paul Orlando, her number one fan, has also been a huge influence.

"I'm a passionate person," he says. "I wasn't a great athlete. I played baseball in high school but I never took to the higher levels. I still work out and I've done martial arts for years. My business is in the USA. After seven years with ADP I started Orlando And Associates Inc. We do engineering project management. As a kid, I played little league and kept playing baseball in high school, but not when I went to University. In karate, I'm a black belt, at the second level. When they were younger, I wanted the girls to train with me, work out with me, so we could do things together. I did it more for me, and they didn't really like it, but they were good at it. I never wanted them to do something they don't love or want to do. It was too competitive for Victoria. That's the big difference between those two girls, in sports and in life. Alex loves to compete. Victoria doesn't like the yelling, screaming, and all the stress that goes with competitive sports. I don't even try to account for the difference between them. I told them as young girls, "If you're going to do it, then do it, and finish it. Do your best. Give it your all." That's the way I was and wanted to instill that in them. "Finish the season," I always said. I don't scream, like some parents. I wanted them to have fun. I live my life the way I train, the way I played ball and did martial arts: with passion."

When he retires, he plans to go to Italy. As for Alex, he has always said, "She's got to go where she wants."

The Victoria Orlando Story

Alexandra says one of the biggest influences in her life was her big sister, Victoria Ann Orlando.

"Ever since I was little I wanted to be exactly like my big sister. Since she was four years older, we didn't get along till much later. I was that annoying bratty little sister, tagging along, hanging on her every word. Don't get me wrong, I loved to bother her and drive her crazy, but no matter what happened I knew she was always there for me."

"As my gymnastics career got more serious she became one of my biggest fans. Growing up she knew how important this was to me and didn't complain when my parents had to miss one of her recitals or important days. I felt guilty every time that happened."

"A lot of my family's time went into my training and competing. I honestly don't know how sometimes she just accepted that without an argument. It was hard for her, obviously, and for her to support me like no one else through all this, makes her one of the most amazing people I know."

"Victoria is my rock. When we were younger we didn't have serious conversations about things going on in our lives, but being able to curl up with her on the couch and having her hold on to me, hugging, meant the world to me. In our own way that was showing how much we cared for each other, even with the age difference and the constant fighting."

"As I got older and we had more things in common, I

started confiding in her about my insecurities as a gymnast and the problems I was facing having to balance everything in my life. She helped me through a lot of times where I thought I just couldn't go on. She constantly reassured me of this incredible talent and passion I had inside of myself, and that I had the power to do anything I wanted to do. She just wanted me to be happy, like a protective older sister would."

"She would do anything for me and I for her. We hate to see each other upset and hurting. She probably doesn't even know this, but I am her biggest fan. Because I'm still the younger one it is my job to annoy her, but deep down I am just in awe of her."

Canada

Nationality and family have also played major parts in the Alexandra Orlando story.

"My parents lived in New York, before moving to Canada, and my family is from Italy. All my relatives live in Italy or the U.S.A. Only my sister and I were born in Canada. They all tease me about being soooo Canadian."

"My family is very American. All my relatives are Italian or American, except for my sister, who is Canadian, like me. My father served in the American army, in Vietnam."

"Everybody in our family loves to tease us about being Canucks," Victoria Orlando says. "Alex is hardcore Canadian. She says 'eh' all the time. I say 'huh'. I tease her about it. Our American cousins tease us because of our accents and our Canadian vocabulary. They think it's very funny when we say things like 'pop' instead of 'soda'. We're called 'the little Canucks'."

"The people in my family all say I am soooo Canadian. We have heated discussions about it. They love how Canadian

I am but they can't understand why I wouldn't compete for the USA. I have dual citizenship. The Americans offered more money for training and competitions. I just can't see myself draped in the flag of any other country but Canada."

"Lots of athletes do switch countries in order to compete. Personally, I'd rather not go to the Olympics than go and compete for any other country. That's how Canadian I am."

"I'm Canadian, not American. I'm not Italian, either. I have family and roots there. I've been in Toronto for my whole life and I've had nothing but amazing experiences here."

"Alex is so Canadian," her father says. "In her heart, Alex is completely Canadian. She'll defend Canada to the death. She has squabbles with her cousins, who are American or Italian. She is always telling them how wonderful it is to be a Canadian."

"I'm such a joke for my family. There's a lot of teasing, especially about being so Canadian. They can't understand it because they're Italian and American. But I was born here, grew up here, I've had so many amazing experiences here, and I've been representing Canada for so long, traveling around the world to compete in my sport."

"My grandma is a bit disappointed in me because I haven't become fluent in Italian. My mother and my grandma speak very proper Italian to each other all the time and I've learned enough to understand them. My father is Sicilian and they consider his Italian to be slang. I love languages and studied French all the way through school. I love going to Montreal and getting along in French. I would love to study abroad for a year while I'm a University of Toronto student, and go to either Italy or Australia."

The last word on the subject of influences should go to Alexandra's father.

"What I love about her so much, and why she's a champion, a true superstar, is that she doesn't have an air about her, like some elite athletes," he says. "She trains with little ones, at the club, and she coaches them, sometimes, too. She is a superstar, but she doesn't act it, and you'd never know it until you see her in training or, even better, competing, particularly at an important event."

Chapter 8. Rhythmic Gymnastics Night In Canada (With Coach's Corner Featuring Dimitritchka "Mimi" Masleva)

"Today, rhythmic gymnastics is witnessing a spectacularly rapid development with young people and an impressive echo from the media and the public. The reasons for this growing success are simple. Rhythmics puts expressive young women on stage, artists who are exhausted simultaneously by the technical handling of the apparatus as well as the perfect mastery of body expression."

~ Gymnastics Canada

Canada's Ritmika Club Versus Palaces Of Sport Around The World

Ritmika, officially known as Ritmika Rhythmic Gymnastics Club, is a good looking, new, clean, spacious gymnastics club located in a new part of Vaughan, just north of Toronto, beside the new Vaughan Mills Shopping Centre. The area is still under construction and roads are so new that nobody seems to know their way around the area, which was farmland a few years ago. The gymnastics club is in a modern building in a row of several identical buildings, which house various businesses and warehouses.

Vaughan, with population 245,000, is a city in York Region north of Toronto and the fastest growing municipality in Canada, having nearly doubled in population since 1991. Vaughan is part of the Greater Toronto Area. Its slogan is 'The City Above Toronto'.

The Great One himself, Wayne Gretzky started his illustrious hockey career as a junior playing for the now defunct Vaughan Nationals hockey team of the Ontario Hockey Association during the 1975-76 season.

Ritmika's location does not look like the kind of neighborhood that would inspire world champions in gymnastics or any other sport except, perhaps, bass fishing. There is no hint that Canadian national champions past and future have trained here, that talent from around the world gathers here to send Canadian athletes to compete around the world. In fact, if you stop your car to ask someone where the gymnastics club is, you will draw only blank stares. Most people in the neighborhood have never even heard of the place or know there is a gymnastics club nearby. Nobody walks the streets in this part of the world - everyone drives a new car - but inside one of the many buildings that looks like the warehouse for a new enterprise, rhythmic gymnasts warm-up, train, and compete, executing all the athletic and balletic moves their sport is famous for, from the level of young beginner to international champions.

An ordinary, unmarked, door, at the side of a nondescript building, dwarfed by the dimensions of what looks like a warehouse, opens into a small foyer decorated with photos, posters, news clippings, and trophies of international rhythmic gymnastics champions. It also has promotional material for yoga classes. Most of the photos, posters, and newspaper accounts are about Ritmika's reigning champion, Alexandra Orlando. Some of them feature the club's future stars. There is no mention of Mary Sanders, except as a former teammate of Alexandra's.

To one side of the reception area, there is a short hallway, decorated with more rhythmic gymnastics posters, leading to a few small offices. Behind the reception area is where the main action of the club takes place.

A row of wooden bleachers and a very large carpet are the two hints the huge room is not an empty warehouse, awaiting truckloads of car parts or computer components. The ceiling is high, but not high enough for the rhythmic gymnasts who work out here, tossing clubs, balls, and hoops, high in the air, waving impossibly long ribbon and short ropes.

It is a clean, well-lighted, space and this private club is the best place in the country dedicated to rhythmic gymnastics, but it pales in comparison to the athletic facilities dedicated to other sports and sometimes shared with rhythmic gymnastics, such as Seneca and Etobicoke. And compared to the palaces of the sport erected in the countries that revere rhythmic gymnastics, it is nothing at all. In Russia and Bulgaria, China and Japan, across Europe, in Australia and Malaysia, even in Venezuela, governments have created incredible facilities dedicated to rhythmic gymnastics.

The palaces of this sport have not just one carpet but several. The ceilings are so high they seem to touch the sky. Coaches work one-on-one with stars and future stars of the rhythmic gymnastics world and physiotherapists, doctors, and sports psychologists are working nearby.

Ritmika has hundreds of young women training for the sport; other countries have thousands.

For a Canadian girl, traveling to Bulgaria for a training camp, or to Venezuela for the Pan American Games, to Italy, Spain, or Portugal for the World Championships, to Australia for the Commonwealth Games, or to Greece or China for the Olympics, it is like Cinderella going to a castle for a ball.

"I wish rhythmic gymnastics was a lot more popular," Alex says. "I wish people understood it better. And I wish people would stop making fun of it, especially on TV and in the movies. I think rhythmic gymnastics competitions should be televised. If chess, poker, and spelling bees can be shown on TV and find an audience, I think rhythmic gymnastics should be given a chance."

"Alex is a big star around the world, but not so much at home, and that's a little disappointing," her mother says. "What's the best way to improve the profile of rhythmic gymnastics in Canada? Win more medals."

"We train 25 or 30 hours a week and nobody appreciates that. They still think it's not a sport because of the costumes, music, and apparatus," Alex says. "The film *Old School* with Will Ferrell didn't help."

In the DreamWorks Pictures movie called *Old School*, the American actor Will Ferrell, formerly of *Saturday Night Live*, gets set on fire, French kisses another man, and performs rhythmic gymnastics in front of a crowd at a funeral.

"It was a funny movie but it didn't do anything for rhythmic gymnastics," Alex says.

Victoria Orlando says, "I loved that movie and it makes Alex furious that I love it. There's a two-minute part at the end of the movie with Will Ferrell in leotards with a ribbon from rhythmic gymnastics, and he prances around, does a weird leap with the ribbon. Everybody now says to Alex, "Oh, you do rhythmic gymnastics like Will Ferrell in *Old School*", and it makes her furious. The part with him doing rhythmic gymnastics is in the preview for the movie, too, so everybody saw it."

"Gymnastics Canada has started putting together four sports for competitions and each one helps attract an audience for the others. We have artistic gymnastics, trampoline, and acro with rhythmic gymnastics, and that helps."

"I wish we could promote the sport better. I hope I helped at the Commonwealth Games by winning a record number of medals."

"We can't get sponsors. We're allowed to have sponsors but they want to be associated with the number one team in the world. Making it into the top 15 in the world is an enormous accomplishment in this sport, but it hasn't been recognized by sponsors."

"There's lots of stuff I'd like to change in rhythmic gymnastics," Marisa Orlando says. "Judging is subjective and political. You need the right backing, including the club and the coach. Also, you really have to shine. You have to get noticed. For all her hard work, dedication, training, success, Alexandra certainly deserves more recognition and so does her sport. It's long overdue."

"When Alex went to Puerto Rico, American gymnasts were also invited, including some who had Olympic medals, and Alex was a crowd favourite. I think it was, in part, because Alex has a Latin look. She could have been one of them."

"That may have signaled the start of something. The little girls at nationals, in Canada, all follow Alex's career and get very excited to see her. She is hugely popular at Ritmika, her home club. The new kids and their parents, in particular, are thrilled to see her and to meet her."

"It has been a whirlwind for Alex ever since she won six gold medals at the Commonwealth Games in Australia. We are still getting calls. We've heard from everyone you can think of - except agents and sponsors."

"Canada is struggling, compared to other countries," Annely Riga says. "Australia is doing well because of the money their government has invested at the grass-roots level, building sports centres. I have one club and there is only so much I can do."

"The winter Olympics gets more funding in Canada than summer sports," Mimi Masleva says. "Figure skating and skiing are strong, in Canada, as well as hockey. It's great that the Winter Olympics will be in Canada in 2010. This is a hockey country. There is nothing wrong with the focus on hockey in Canada. Everybody plays. But there are other sports to focus on, for girls, especially, including rhythmic gymnastics. We should give other sports room to grow."

"Rhythmic gymnastics is so misunderstood," Victoria Orlando says. "People still don't understand it. They seem to think rhythmic gymnasts are just dancers who can lift their legs higher. I don't know how to advertise it. We need more television coverage. It's ridiculous we don't get it, except on random cable channels. There should be a commercial for nationals. Sometimes you see snippets of coverage of rhythmic gymnastics on the news. When you watch it, how could you not love it? Also, you can see how hard the girls work. People will be amazed. It's crazy what they can do and it's pretty. People need to see it."

"If there were five girls like Alex in Canada, it would be better for the sport. They need a group, competing together, to do really well. In Canada, people still don't know the sport or the difference between rhythmic gymnastics and artistic gymnastics."

"I like watching the younger girls, there's a lot of really strong girls. Right now Canada's not making the kind of impression people expect internationally. Our top three are really great and the girls coming up are strong. I hope the senior girls will be coaches."

"One of my favourite things is when the little girls come to see the seniors and they get so excited to see Alex.

People go crazy. Five-year-olds want autographs. They really look up to her for what she has accomplished in their sport and she's a nice girl, approachable."

"I love hockey. Canada has lots of very talented, wonderful guys and girls, but I think we should give some of the money they get to other sports. I'd like to see them put some of their salaries to other sports."

Paul Orlando says, "The problem is that it's not a contact sport. It looks like a contact sport, sometimes, when they are all together on the carpet, warming up before a competition. Alex got hurt several times. Once, she got hit in eye with club and almost lost it. They should combine her sport with artistic gymnastics or something to make them all more popular."

"To make rhythmic gymnastics and other sports more popular in Canada, they are amalgamating them. Gymnastics Canada is changing their events so that tumbling, trampoline, rhythmic gymnastics and artistic gymnastics are all together."

"The Canadian team is getting much better. We are now ranked 14th in the world. Breaking into the top 15 in this sport, dominated by the Eastern Europeans, is quite remarkable. I believe we'll be in the top ten, next year."

"There are lots of great young girls coming up in Canada. There may be a gap for a few years. The younger girls need to travel more to gain international experience. After all, this is a judged sport, and in order to be judged you have to be seen. That means lots of travel and lots of competitions, so the judges can see you again and again."

Coach's Corner, With Dimitritchka "Mimi" Masleva

"Please keep watching rhythmic gymnastics in spite of its situation. If you quit watching it, rhythmic gymnastics will not exist

any longer. Your eyes are much more important than judges are."
~Teodora Alexandrova, from Bulgaria

"Keep your fingers crossed for Beijing," Dimitritchka "Mimi" Masleva says. "I am looking forward to going to that city. It is the greatest city in China. Alex deserves to go there and she will do well."

"We have a good chance to qualify for the Olympics, based on our ranking during the year, as Alex has moved up from 18th, to 17th, to 16th, and is still training hard," Mimi says. "Soon she will be 13th in the world, I believe."

"Also, there is a new way of doing the rankings, with more emphasis on the second competition, with the apparatus, and that is Alex's strength."

"Even so, it is hard to compete with the former Soviet countries as they are so strong and have a 60-year tradition of excellence in this sport."

"One of Alex's competitors is from Mexico and Alex was better than her, but the Mexican girl has been training in Russia, putting in many hours. It costs 200 Euros per day."

"My dream of having two Olympians didn't happen. But I still believed. Working hard and being positive is the way to make it happen. I would love for this to happen for Alex as she really deserves it. She should have gone to the last Olympics."

"If the Soviet Union was still one country, Alex would win an Olympic medal, but now she has to compete against all those countries that used to be part of the Soviet Union."

"Alex would win in ribbons, at the very least. Technically she is the best in the world with ribbons. She is also very good with clubs. Ribbons are her favourite apparatus, I believe, and that's a very good thing because it is the ribbons that often decide competitions. It is very long and it is hard to keep the ribbon up, off the floor, all the time, and to execute the turns, which are compulsory, and Alex's turns are very strong."

Coaching And Communism

"I am a lucky coach. I was the Bulgarian national coach for six years and had a happy group that included gold medals and world champions."

"I felt it was too much so I said I wanted to do something else, other than coach at the international level. So, the government sent me to Japan. We were still under the communist system. A company in Japan wanted a coach to work with their team. I was there eight years and they qualified for the Olympics in Atlanta. And then I said "enough is enough". I worked with the Chinese as well as the Japanese. And then I came here. I speak English, Bulgarian, and Japanese. Where you live, you learn the language."

"After ten years here, we have national champions, Mary went to the last Olympics, and Alex is aiming for the next Olympics."

"Coaching in Canada and Japan never crossed my mind when I was in Bulgaria."

"The changes in Bulgaria, since I left, have been amazing."

"My mother and my oldest son are still there and I try to go back every year. I took Mary and Alex to camps in Bulgaria because they have excellent facilities and it is less expensive there. I still know lots of people in the sport and was able to make arrangements and get help. Alex has worked with their three-time world champion. We invited her to work with Alex, and she agreed, as she likes Alex. It is good for us to get a new view. She helped us change a routine or two. Maria Petrovia, the Bulgarian star."

"In Bulgaria and the former Soviet countries, every medal is paid. If you win a medal in international competition, you get a government salary."

"In the communist era, we lived in a closed society, but the government took very good care of us, called us The Golden Girls, and were very open to the idea of having us travel all over the world for competitions."

"Now, the Bulgarians have found a lot of sponsors for their team."

"Russia has lots of money for this sport. When we compete against them, they are always amazed at what we have done because they know we do not even have a proper gym, in Canada."

"Also, in Russia, one coach works with one athlete. Here, it is very intensive, the way we have to work. If I could work one-on-one with Alex, exclusively, she would be ten times better and three steps ahead."

"Mary, Alex, never got the star treatment at our club. They trained along with the other girls. Sometimes I could put Mary and Alex with Carly and Nathalie in a group for some exercises, but that was it."

"There is no magical sponsor for rhythmic gymnastics in Canada."

The Controversy Over The Last Olympics
"Alex has done a great job. She missed the last Olympics by one spot. It was a very difficult situation. She was in the best shape at the worlds, but they took competition one for the qualification instead of competition two."

"Usually, if you are 21st in the world, you are going to

the Olympics. Alex was almost ready to quit but she is a fighter, inside, and also very ambitious and intelligent."

"I've always told her that the judges in our sport cannot be controlled so you have to live with them. The only thing you can do is train hard and move to a higher level of difficulty. That's what Alex decided to do after getting so close to going to the Olympics."

"Alex has a very strong character. She is strong inside. She never gives up. I admire her for her persistence."

"There is no other way than to train harder. When Alex was disappointed by judges or by the decision about not going to the Olympics, she knew there was only one thing to do: train harder and at a higher level of difficulty."

"It was disappointing for me, too. It was my dream, to have two Olympians from Canada in rhythmic gymnastics."

"Alex and Mary trained in the same gym with me all the time. The three of us traveled around all year with Alex competing for Canada and Mary competing for the USA."

"When the COC decided to fund athletes who were in the top 12 in the world, Mary made her decision to join the American team. Alex chose to stay. I told them both, all the time, these are personal decisions so you choose for yourself and no matter what you choose I am with you."

"Mary got huge support from the USA."

"My plan was to have two gymnasts at the Olympics. They were both so good. They practiced four hours per day and they were competitive with the Europeans who practiced seven hours a day. Mary and Alex were still going to school, attending high school in Toronto, but their competition trained all day and did not go to school."

"For two years, we were traveling to the biggest international competitions, with Alex competing for the Canadians and Mary competing for the Americans. When I was with Alex, I was the official coach for Canada. When I was with Mary, I was her personal coach. Sometimes the Americans did not send a coach, so I would be the official coach for the Americans, too."

"The American judges fought hard for Mary. Judging is political and the Americans were able to do things for Mary at this level. All the judges support their own country."

"Mary did no training in the USA. She helped all Canadian gymnasts by training in our club."

The Alex And Mary Story

"Mary and Alex are very different. Mary had a gentle, sensitive style. Alex's style was fire. She touches you with every move. It is more of a Bulgarian style that I tried to give her. I encouraged Mary and Alex to have different styles, to develop their own styles. We didn't want them to be the same."

"They had different ways of working with me, too. From the start, Mary always trusted me 100 percent. Alex is the same, now, but our relationship was all about fighting - in a good way. We had disagreements, in the past, but Alex would always do it my way, in the end. She always asked me, "Why do we have to repeat the same thing so many times?" - Now she understands. It is easy for us to work together now."

"Alex always had this fire inside of her. You could tell there was something inside of her. I brought it out. I don't say I'm the best coach in Canada. I say I am always trying to encourage the athletes to be themselves. My international experience helps."

"Alex and Mary moved to our club when Alex was a junior and Mary was a senior. Alex became junior champion and Mary was senior champion."

"In the beginning, they were not so creative, but the creativity developed over the years."

"After the Olympics, Mary went with Cirque de Soleil, but after one year, she was ready to come back home."

"Marisa Orlando supported Mary, as well as Alex. Mary's father died. In our sport, in Canada, you have to pay for everything. Alex's mom helped Mary with travel expenses. It was good for Alex, too, to have Mary there. Mary is a couple of years older than Alex and was always one step ahead of her, so she was a good influence and showed her the way to the next step, again and again."

"When Mary joined the American team, there was a lot of publicity, and it helped us by giving some attention to the Canadian team."

The Future Of Rhythmic Gymnastics

"We have some excellent girls coming up. Carly Orava is very good and has changed a great deal in the past three years. Working with top gymnasts has helped her develop quickly. Judges ask me, "What did you do to her? She's changed so much, so fast!"

"Natalie Ngo is amazing. She is a pleasure to work with, as she is a workaholic. Technically, she is very strong. And she is also very artistic."

"In Europe, girls stay in this sport until they are women. They are still competing at age 24, 25, 26 …. Canadians don't want to stay so long."

"Rhythmic gymnastics is very good for athletes. It teaches discipline."

"For me, the music is the most important thing. My strength is that I feel the music very well. In rhythmic gymnastics, every beat of the music has to be synchronized with a movement or the apparatus. Every move has to attract the eye. It's very demanding."

"Alex is very good with the music. She is a good singer, too, like her sister, although she never sings in public. We travel together so much, I've heard her sing. She's good."

Rhythmic Gymnastics In Canada

It is too bad this sport has not received enough attention in Canada. The best facility is in Etobicoke. We make use of Seneca's facilities, at times, when they can give us a few hours. We work out of a private club. It has high ceilings, but they are not high enough. It has a carpet, but it is only a half carpet. We have to go outside the country to train, to get a bigger gym. Our sport gets no support from Ontario or Canada. Our athletes would be much better if their training facilities were just a little bit better."

"China and Japan have built amazing facilities. That's the way to create an Olympic champion. Australia has created three high performance centres. Canada does not have one. Soon we will be out of the picture. It is sad, because we have the talent, but not the facilities. Very soon, Canada will disappear, in rhythmic gymnastics. I'm a very positive person. I dream and believe, but that's the reality."

"I'm going to miss these kids, Alex and Mary, Carly and Nathalie. I'm not going to coach at the international level, after this. I would love to work with the little kids. That makes me happy. It's very challenging."

Chapter 9. Diets And Disorders: Sacrificing Pizza, Pasta, And Boyfriends

(When asked if the Russian team was doping) "We and doping? We take only vitamins". But there was one very funny case. At the World Youth games they told to the small girls that they will make a doping control for chocolate, baked things and coca cola. They believed and got frightened. They came crying to me and asked, "Alina, will they disqualify us? We ate something...."

~Alina Kabayeva,
from "The Sports Life in Russia" Magazine

(After the 1994 World Championships where she became World Champion for second year in a row, when asked what she had eaten that day) "Two apples. I think."

~Maria Petrova

"The sacrifices Alex has made for her sport are unbelievable," her father, Paul Orlando, says. "She craves pizza and pasta but never touches them. Once in a while, she eats, and the next day the coach says, "You gained a pound!" Since she was small, my rule was, "you gotta eat". I told her, "If I find out you're throwing up, it's all over."

A shocking expose was written on the treatment of young competitive female gymnasts and figure skaters by Joan Ryan called <u>Little Girls In Pretty Boxes</u>. It covered the trials and tribulations of Kerri Strug, Dominique Moceanu, and others. In her book, <u>Little Girls in Pretty Boxes: *The Making and*</u>

Breaking of Elite Gymnasts and Figure Skaters, Ryan discusses how performers such as Michelle Kwan and Tara Lipinski suffered starvation diets and psychological abuse by fame-crazed coaches and families.

Her book is a powerful plea to end the obsession some nations seem to have about winning at any cost. Little Girls in Pretty Boxes describes the horrors endured by girls at the hands of their coaches and their own families. The book has already helped reform Olympic sports. Ryan has updated it to reflect the latest developments in women's gymnastics and figure skating.

Mary Sanders has been quoted as saying she thinks there is a lot of pressure on gymnasts to be a certain weight and a lot of girls get stressed and get injured, so they might take something. She said that is where the use of diuretics comes into place. She also said she did not think it was as popular in rhythmic gymnastics as the scandals going on in figure skating. She noted that the Eastern Europeans dominate rhythmic gymnastics and not only are they very talented but they train eight hours a day. Their lives are different as they do not go to school, as North Americans do, and they completely focus on their sport.

"I didn't have any weight issues when I started out, as a little girl, because I was tiny and thin. However, with puberty, I shot up quickly, got tall quite fast, and then my weight became a bit of a problem for a while," Alex says. "Girls that age are very sensitive. When I was 13 and 14, it was very hard for me. If anyone made the smallest comment about my weight or size, I'd take it very personally, worry about it, get frustrated, and drive my parents crazy. I tried dieting and now I hate diets because, in my experience, you lose some weight and then you gain twice as much."

"I found it very hard to train and diet at the same time. Lots of girls retire due to the difficulty of doing those two things at the same time. It is so hard to worry about your weight and focus on your training at the same time. It's very hard to compete when you're busy worrying about your weight. You see lots of eating disorders in this sport, in gymnastics generally, and other sports."

"I'm on the more muscular side, compared to the others in the top 15, internationally, but my muscles are toned, not bulging, and it looks nice when I'm on the carpet and on TV. Working out and training, in the gym and at the club, you gain a lot of muscle. Artistic gymnasts are all muscle and they look great."

"I've worked with personal trainers, for fitness, and they never seem to understand my concerns. They say, "You have zero body fat, so what are you worried about?" But I have to worry about my size because "looks" are such an important part of this sport."

"Now that I'm older, I feel I'm far beyond all those old worries I had when I was 13 or 14. I know how to lose weight."

"In this sport, the way you look is very important. The Europeans are too thin, in my opinion. I always want to be healthy. I eat healthy. I don't eat bread, pasta, or pizza, or anything with carbohydrates. I like bread, pasta, and pizza, but I don't eat them. Because of my Italian background, family, and friends, I'm tempted to eat pasta and pizza all the time, but I just remind myself I have the rest of my life to enjoy food the way they do. I eat a lot of salad. For protein, I eat a balance of meat, eggs, and fish. You have to sacrifice to be successful at this level."

"When I cheat, I eat a little bit of chocolate. I love chocolate!"

In her teens, Alexandra experienced all the distractions most adolescents meet.

"We lose many girls at that stage," her coach says. "They ask themselves, "Why sweat for hours in the gym when I could be making friends and having fun with them?"

"It is a well-known fact that eating disorders exist, especially within the Russian team, for our sport. It was true especially in the Communist era, when their coaches were free to do whatever they wanted with their athletes and the completely controlled them," Mimi says.

"When Alex hit adolescence, it was hard for her. She grew quickly and it was hard for her to get in shape again. She gained some weight and had to lose it. By the time she competed at the 2006 Commonwealth Games, she was in great shape."

"Judges don't say anything to the athletes about the way they look, but they do talk to the coaches. They say, "Why is she in this kind of shape?" Like ballerinas and figure skaters, if you want to be at the top of the sport, you have to look a certain way."

"Now Alex takes care of her weight and shape with a fitness program that includes Pilates. I hope she doesn't gain any weight. I hope she can stay the way she is."

"Alex likes to eat, but she is more mature now than at the start of adolescence."

"We haven't had anyone with the problem of being too thin here. We have problems at the other end of the spectrum. The Russians tend to be tall, thin, and muscular. The Japanese are strong competitors but their body type isn't as ideal for this sport. Long arms, long legs, looks better, in rhythmic gymnastics, just as it does in ballet. You have to be born a certain way."

"Food is always an issue. It has been a big issue for

Alex. We know a few girls who have struggled with anorexia and bulimia. Alex hasn't had those problems. She loves to eat. She's being so good, watching what she eats, not eating too much, eating the right things, staying away from pizza and pasta," her mother says. "It makes a difference when she walks onto the carpet."

Her mother adds, "She is the thinnest and the best shape ever, right now. That is because she has been working out in a gym and she never did that before, although she always trained a great deal for her sport. She believes you need to work out, as well as train, and that's the whole package. This year, while she was living in residence at the University of Toronto, her coach told her to go home, to eat, for a few weeks."

"Residence, in first year of University, was the best thing for Alex. She got to meet so many other people her own age who were not in her sport. I saw her as having a much more normal life, for a change. Most of the friends she made were athletes. They understand and support each other. They watched Alex, to see if she was eating enough."

Boyfriends

"I'm a romantic person," Alexandra says. " I believe in love at first sight, meeting someone and falling in love, but that hasn't happened to me yet. I believe having a boyfriend would be almost impossible for me with my schedule, training so much of the time and traveling every month. However, if I did fall head-over-heels in love, I'd find a way to make it work. It's hard to be romantic when you're so crazy busy."

Lots of girls quit competing and give up on their athletic careers because of boyfriends, she says, or just because of the desire to socialize - to go to parties with friends.

"Our coaches often ask us, 'Do you have a boyfriend?' "I'm not anti-social or anything, but I haven't fallen head-over-heals in love so I haven't had to try to fit a boyfriend into my busy life, yet."

"There have been no boys in the picture," Marisa Orlando says. "That's just starting. It's all women, at all these rhythmic gymnastics events. You don't meet boys. She went to an all-girls school, for high school. That was true until Alex went to the Pacific Games, the Pan American Games, and the Commonwealth Games, and the Canadian women traveled with the Canadian male athletes."

"That was a new and fun experience for me," she adds.

It turns out that Alex the Great, formerly a tomboy, has another side to her, too.

Girly Girls

"Most of my friends are athletes," Alex says. "I have a few artistic friends, too. I had more artistic friends in high school - people who were painters and writers. When I'm with friends who are not athletes, sometimes I feel as though I'm not normal. The things they do seem normal and I don't do many of those things. Sometimes I feel like they don't understand what I'm going through, but they make me feel like a normal teenager. I don't know what I would do without them. Sometimes it is good to get away from anything related to sports and competition for a while."

Alex sounds quite normal when she says, "I also have friends who are "girly girls"."

Girly girls?

"I'm a big girly girl, at times," she confesses. "I love working out at the gym, and I'm sure I'll keep it up for my whole life, but I also love to shop and to dress up, too. People are surprised to find that out about me. They are used to seeing me at the gym, all sweaty and without make-up. The truth is, gymnasts dress up more than others when they go out. Maybe it's because they wear sweatpants and sweatshirts so much of the time. It's a nice change."

Alex's new friends at the University of Toronto had to coach her on how to "dress down".

"I went to a rugby game a little while ago because some friends invited me to see Canada play against England, and they felt they had to tell me not to dress up because it was a rugby game," she says. "Dress down, they told me. They were laughing at me because they know I like to dress up whenever there's a reason."

Of course, dressing up, wearing costumes and make-up, is part of her sport. Athletes competing in rhythmic gymnastics dress more and more like female ice skaters.

"I love clothes and make-up and that's important in my sport. You have to be poised and "proper" as well as very athletic. It's a weird balance," she says.

"The 'costumes' we wear are something else. There's nothing like them, except the outfits figure skaters wear. I don't like the word 'costume'. I always say 'competition suit'."

Las Vegas Costumes Worn By Rhythmic Gymnasts

Creating a 'competition suit' is a long process, Alex reveals. "It starts with my coach and her ideas. We discuss them. Our ideas are given to a designer, who makes up several samples for us to look at. We look at them to find out what's flattering, what will make me look smaller, rather than bigger, and what colours look the best with my complexion. Next, seamstresses create new samples, without sequins. Actually, I don't use sequins. I prefer crystals. They are more sophisticated."

On each competition suit, there are a thousand crystals. "The suits cost over one thousand dollars each because they are handmade and the crystals are glued on by hand."

Although she sometimes feels she isn't normal, when she is with friends who are not competitive athletes, but when she is with other rhythmic gymnasts, she feels completely at home.

"I feel I have the best of both worlds," she says, "My girly girl side is balanced with my sports side."

"I admire all the women in the top 15. Very few of them are prima donas, but there are a few. My favourite gymnast to watch is Elizabeth Paisieva, from Bulgaria. She looks beautiful, on the floor, and is just stunning to watch. They all have admirable technical skills."

"We believe that to be in the top 15 in my sport, you have to look European."

Alex made it through that stage somehow. I think it is because she knew she was good at her sport and could go far with it. Also, as she says, very maturely, she has the rest of her life to experience all those other things so it's a good idea to keep her focus on her sport right now.

Alex knows what she wants and she knew all along that this is what she wanted, even though it's nothing but hard work. Learning to prioritize is part of their training. "I have my whole life to do all that. Ask any parent of an adolescent: teenagers say things they don't mean. I said things to my mom I wish I had never said. If you write those things down in your journal instead of saying them out loud to someone, it doesn't do any damage."

Chapter 10. High School Confidential: Woman's World

"High school is a scary place," Alex says. "I switched schools quite a bit before high school and then went to Havergal for four years, from grade 9 to 12."

Havergal College is a leading independent boarding and day school for girls in Toronto.

Founded in 1894 by Ellen Knox, and named after Frances Ridley Havergal, the school has many prominent alumni. Notable 'Old Girls' or alumnae, include:

* Dr Carolyn Bennett, a Liberal Member of Parliament;
* Former New Brunswick Lieutenant-Governor Margaret Norrie McCain;
* Dora Mavor Moore, Canadian theatre pioneer;
* Ruth Atkinson Hindmarsh, social welfare advocate;
* Kate Reid, actress;
* Margot Kidder, actress;
* Rachel Blanchard, actress;
* Gillian Apps, Canadian women's hockey team, 2004 Olympic gold medallist;
* and Alexandra Orlando.

"Havergal was amazingly supportive," Marisa Orlando says. "We learned from Mary that the public school system may not be as supportive as a private school. Havergal was happy to re-schedule tests, assignments, whatever; teachers put in extra hours and met with Alex at odd hours, morning or after school; and the guidance counselors were amazing. She won their award for being excellent inside and outside of the school. They gave it to her two years in a row. Her marks have always been excellent. She is the most disciplined kid I know. I'm in awe of her. We all are. She's so special."

Alex's father says, "Her high school years were challenging but Havergal was great. They supported her like you wouldn't believe. They realized she had talent and they encouraged her to develop it. They tutored her, so she could keep up with classes, even if it meant being there at six or seven in the morning to make up for exams or get extra help. They stayed late, if needed. Alex did quite well there and I thought it was far superior to the public schools."

"After Grade Five, she left public school because it didn't support her. One year at a public school, Alex missed a lot of classes, as she was traveling the world to compete in rhythmic gymnastics, and the best the school could do was give her an average mark. For her mark, they gave her the class average. Alex has always been at the top of the class, so she didn't like that. Private school also taught her time management and how to study."

The program at Havergal is both challenging and stimulating, they claim. They seek to exceed the expectations of the Ontario Ministry of Education, in English, math, science, humanities and social sciences, as well as classical studies, dramatic and visual arts, information and communication technology, modern languages, music, religious education and physical education.

They claim girls thrive in a cooperative and collaborative learning environment.

"Our approach to learning is based on substantial research about how girls learn best which indicates that, in a single-sex classroom, girls show more confidence, participating fully in class, tackling problems and expressing ideas. They demonstrate greater willingness to take risks and are more likely to pursue advanced studies in math and science," Havergal claims.

With the focus on the development of the individual as a whole, Havergal's program supports All-around education and is enriched by co-curricular activities designed to meet the interests of every student. Students pursue their individual talents and interests through music, performing and visual arts programs, high-calibre athletics activities and participation in clubs and school life.

"I went to Havergal because it's a private school that understands the demands of the sports world," Alexandra says. "My teachers helped me a lot with all the stress involved in being on a national team, traveling a lot, and meeting the demands of the provincial curriculum. My teachers were great."

Every student from Junior Kindergarten to Senior Year is encouraged to develop leadership skills and a commitment to community service. In addition to elected positions on student council, sports teams and clubs, a House system provides valuable opportunities for girls to be leaders and to make a difference by participating in community service.

This is the Havergal Vision:

"In this age of instant and global communication, young women must think critically and creatively, make thoughtful and logical decisions, facilitate change and solve problems. They must be willing to stand by their own decisions and stand up for others. They must be innovative and persistent, respect differences, explore opportunities for learning at every stage of life and, perhaps most importantly, have strong personal values. At Havergal, we prepare young women not only to succeed in the 21st century, but to make a difference in their chosen pursuits by enabling each girl to develop her full intellectual, creative, spiritual and physical potential."

Their slogan is 'It's a woman's world'.

They say the Havergal difference is intentional focus on these values and commitments. "Each person at Havergal contributes in a unique way to this difference and each will articulate what this difference means in a unique way. This difference can be heard in our hallways, at Prayers, at athletic competitions, while participating in community service and while taking a moment to reflect on Havergal's place in the global community," they claim on their website.

"It is the spirit and enthusiasm demonstrated for the efforts of each member of the Havergal community. It is the community itself, comprised of people who value excellence and recognize that through effort comes achievement. It is our proud commitment to our history, values and traditions."

"I wish I could have been more involved in high school life, including high school sports," Alexandra says.

"High school was a crazy time, in terms of time management, but I've got it down, now," she says.

"The award Alex received at Havergal is called "Beyond the Ivy"," Marisa Orlando says, "and it is awarded to a student who achieves excellence in her academics and outside of school."

"Grades ten and 11 were the hardest years of high school because of peer pressure about parties, socializing, dating, friends .... I had to learn to balance those desires with my drive to get on the podium," Alex says.

She has developed some real insight into adolescence

and the high school years.

"It's hard to deal with all the changes that happen to you and around you while you're in high school," she says. "You have to find ways to be successful socially and academically, have friends and an identity while getting the grades you need to get accepted into University."

"In high school, you want the best of both worlds: you want to be popular, get high marks, and excel in something. I had the greatest time in high school and it was primarily because I had a passion for my sport."

"Guys aren't that different than girls, when it comes to feeling the pressures of high school life," she claims. "They throw away their athletic careers in order to be cool in high school."

While she was a high school student, Alex traveled across Canada and around the world with her sport, competing in the Berlin World Cup, the Canadian Championships, Pacific Alliance Championships in Burnaby, the Tournament of Corbeil-Essones in France, Berlin Masters, the Zhulietta Shishmanova Memorial in Bulgaria, and the Moscow Grand Prix.

"I've been traveling to Europe for competitions since I was 12-years-old," Alex says, as though it's something any high school student could handle.

She became the Canadian Rhythmic Gymnastics Champion, the Pacific Alliance winner, and then went to the 2006 Commonwealth Games in Australia, where she won six gold medals.

Not bad for a kid in high school!

When she was an adolescent, she was not typical. She was so busy, training and traveling to competitions, she didn't have time for the usual adolescent interests.

"I let her lash out at me, in those years, if she had a bad day," her mother says. "When she was finished, I'd get her to breathe deeply, and then we would talk about whatever was upsetting her. We talked for hours and hours in the car, driving back and forth to the club and the airport. I tried to figure out all her complaints. I tried to help her with her daily problems of gym and school as she tried to keep up with everything. I had to coach her on how to work with her coach. If she lashed out at the coach, or tried to argue, well, it didn't work that way."

"I've had a lot of changes in my life since I was 16, and that was just three years ago," Alex says, looking back on her high school days. "Fortunately, I've had fantastic support from my family, my club, and the provincial and national gymnastics organizations. Everybody wants me to go for it. I know exactly what I want and how to balance the things in my life so I can get there."

"At age 20, Alex doesn't need me nearly as much as when she was younger," her mother notes. "She keeps doing everything she needs to do to compete on her own."

"Alex's room will be our trophy room after she moves out. She has so many medals, plaques, photos, and mementos from competitions. We have to keep our other daughter in mind, so we won't be turning the living room into a trophy room. Alex's room will be filled with awards."

Chapter 11. Varsity Freedom: Normal Life At Last

"At the University of Toronto, in Woodsworth College, my friends are all athletes, by coincidence," Alexandra says.

"A lot of them tease me about what I eat," Alex says. "Some of them have competitions to see who can eat the most. Most varsity athletes I know have to bulk up, especially the football players. Or else they have incredible metabolisms - they're soooo lucky! When I eat with them, it's very funny, as I have a little salad, with something for protein, and they act like they're at an all-you-can-eat restaurant. In first year, my roommate was a swimmer, on the varsity team, and that worked out well, because we were both keeping crazy hours, training in the morning, going to classes all day, and studying all night, sometimes. I have a great group of friends at school, now."

"This is the most normal her life has been since she started rhythmic gymnastics," Marisa Orlando says. "Living away from home with a lot of people who are like her and support her has been great."

"The University of Toronto has been great," her father says. "Alex loves the school. They're very supportive of her demanding schedule, too."

"I always thought that I would be a doctor, but in high school I realized I didn't have the passion needed to be competitive in medical school," Alex says. "In Grade 12, I took all three sciences and two maths and applied to Commerce at University of Toronto because I believed it was prestigious. It's not an exact fit for me, I've discovered. My dad and our relatives are all in business. I have an uncle who's a stockbroker on Wall Street and I had a good time visiting him while he was working. I'm getting more interested in Political Science, for Peace And Conflict studies. My travels around the world for my sport have made me think about Political Science."

She has changed a lot since her days at Havergal College.

"I took a law course in high school and enjoyed that. I didn't like to write, while I was in high school, and I hated public speaking, but now I like to write and I love big discussions."

She loves the University experience so much, she does not want to miss a year for any reason - not even to go to the Olympic Games.

Tests and exams will not stop Alex from making her way to the top. She often finds herself feeling physically drained from her long commutes to and from her club and her school, not to mention from doing required readings for her courses. However, she always finds time to train, no matter how demanding her schedule. She has managed to find a balance between books and ribbon.

She travels over an hour each way, from Ritmika to the U of T. After a day full of classes, she makes her way up to Ritmika, the rhythmic gymnastics club, for further training.

She is also a part-time gymnastics coach.

She trains about six days a week for four hours each time. It's a lot of work and it's a lot of hours, but it certainly paid off at the Commonwealth Games.

The trip to Australia was difficult because of the competition's timing. Competing is bound to get in the way of your schoolwork, she knows. The Commonwealth Games came at a particularly bad time of the year as second semester exams were coming up.

Learning to use the traveling time to her benefit has helped Alex get her studying done. After winning six gold medals at the Commonwealth Games in Australia, she studied on the plane ride back to Canada.

Would she do it all again, the same way? Almost!

"I'm very excited about next year," she says. "I'm staying in school, with a reduced course load, even though it's time for Olympic qualification. I love learning."

Orlando is moving near her campus and registering as a part-time student, which she hopes will lighten her load.

Chapter 12. Alex the Great And The Dangers Of Rhythmic Gymnastics

The newspaper headlines in Melbourne called her "Alex The Great" after she dominated the 2006 Commonwealth Games in Australia, winning six gold medals, tying the Commonwealth record, and being named Canada's flag bearer for the closing ceremonies. The headline said: "Alexandra The Great All-Around champion."

Her father has been calling her Alex the Great since she was a very young rhythmic gymnast.

Many athletes have cool nicknames but very few athletes have the term 'the great' attached to them. Wayne Gretzky is known as 'The Great One'. Muhammad Ali is known as 'The Greatest Of All Time'. And Tiger Woods is included in this category as the greatest golfer.

By wild coincidence, there is also a stallion known as Alex the Great. A racehorse in the Czech Republic goes by that name. It is in the bloodline of the famous Canadian racehorse Northern Dancer and has won over a half a million dollars so far.

Alex And Alexander The Great

The name Alex the Great alludes to Alexander the Great, also known as Alexander III, who was king of Macedon (336-323 BC). He is considered one of the most successful military commanders in history, conquering most of his known world. Alexander the Great never lost a battle during 11 years of fighting against mostly numerically superior forces.

As the first military commander to attempt to conquer the known world, Alexander integrated infantry, cavalry, and engineers with logistics and intelligence support in a manner never before seen or experienced. Through his efforts to unite East and West he changed the world by introducing advanced Greek political, military, and economic practices throughout the regions he conquered.

Alexander The Great conquered the Persian Empire, including Syria, Phoenicia, Gaza, Egypt, and Mesopotamia. He extended the boundaries of his empire as far as the Punjab.

The similarities are remarkable. Alex the Great, like Alexander, is considered one of the most skilled rhythmic gymnasts in history. She always finished near the top in over a decade of battles, always fighting against numerically superior forces. She integrates engineers with intelligence in a manner never before seen or experienced. She unites the East and the West, competing in the Far East and the West, as well as Eastern Europe and Western Europe, and her background is Italian while her foreground is Canadian. She has already conquered the Commonwealth.

Alexandra Orlando In Literature

The name Alexandra Orlando has an interesting connection to the world of literature, as well.

In the famous novel by Virginia Woolf called Orlando, first published in 1928, the main character is named Orlando and he falls in love with a woman named Alexandra.

If they had married, her name would have been Alexandra Orlando.

A film adaptation of the novel was made in 1993, starring Tilda Swinton as Orlando and Quentin Crisp as Queen

Elizabeth I.

Orlando is considered one of the most readable novels by Woolf, and one of the most influential books of all time, written by a female author. It mixes fiction with biography. It is the story of a young man named Orlando, born in England during the reign of Elizabeth I, who decides not to grow old. He doesn't, and he passes through the ages as a young man until, oddly, he wakes up one morning to find that he has metamorphosed into a woman. He, or she, is the same person, with the same personality and intellect, but in a woman's body. The remaining centuries up to the time the book was written are seen through a woman's eyes. Apart from being, at the beginning of the book, a knightly young man, ready for adventure, Woolf's Orlando takes little from a pseudo-historical hero of the same name.

A project on the history of women's writing in the British Isles was named after the book: The Orlando Project. Orlando: Women's Writing in the British Isles from the Beginnings to the Present is a rich resource for readers with an interest in literature, women's writing, and cultural history.

The Dangers Of Rhythmic Gymnastics

There is a brutal side to this sport that looks so beautiful performed by Alex Orlando and other athletes in rhythmic gymnastics, and it has nothing to do with judging, the competitions, or major events, including the Olympics.

"Warm-ups are notoriously brutal," Alex says. "I've been whacked on the back during warm-ups. I think it was an accident. Somebody could get killed on the carpet during warm-ups. It took two years for me to push myself onto the carpet during warm-ups. I used to warm up in a corner, where nobody would run into me. Now I claim my spot in the middle. The warm-ups were always the worst part. They were horrible. The worst time was my first Grand Prix, which is for the top competitors from the different countries. I was 16 and it was my first time at a competition all by myself, with no teammates, surrounded by all the world leaders in the sport. I was nervous to be the gym with them. When I got on the carpet for my warm-up, there was a mad frenzy. They were ruthless. The middle of the floor was crazy. I stayed in the corner. Now I get right out there and I'll whack them if they don't get out of the way. It's so competitive."

"It's not deliberate whacking, but if you aren't willing to get in there and mix it up you won't get any carpet time before your competition. You have to suck it up and not be a little princess."

Perhaps rhythmic gymnastics would be more popular in a hockey-crazy country like Canada, if the warm-ups were shown on television, as well as the competitions.

Chapter 13. Another Side Of Alex Orlando: An Insider's Report

We asked Alex's big sister, Victoria, to give us the inside scoop, to show us a side of Alexandra Orlando nobody else gets to see, at home, outside of the gym, hanging out with friends, doing the things normal teenagers do.

Victoria Orlando says, "I think it is so important for people to hear her story and find out what she has faced."

"I watched my sister and my mother. I was the outside objective observer. I saw my sister and everything she went through, and my mom, too. The stress was enormous on my mom, at different times. Whatever my sister went through, my mom went through, too. She was always talking to coaches and dealing with judges."

"When or if they make a movie about Alex, based on this book, my mother's part could be played by Diane Lane or maybe by Meryl Streep - someone who can be either tough or very loving, depending on circumstance. My dad is like both Robert Deniro and Dustin Hoffman in *Meet The Fockers*. He's a cross between those two characters, tough and soft, but darker skinned."

"When I have kids, I'll put them in rhythmic gymnastics only if they want to be in it. Maybe they'll say they want to do what their aunt Alex did. I'll support them. I had a great role model for that. I'm totally set to do it. My mother has been amazing."

"It's not easy to be our mother. I can see, now that I'm

older. Imagine having two daughters and one's an athlete but the other one's more into the arts. She had to find a way to balance it all. I felt it was balanced. There were times gym had to come first. I was always included in everything they did and I had my own things. Dad and I became buddies when my mom traveled with my sister. We used to watch action movies together. I was a daddy's girl. I loved action movies as much as he did. We got to hang out together a lot and I liked that."

The Early Years

"Mom was vice president for the gym where Alex trained. She was so involved and active in rhythmic gymnastics, but was always there for me, and in tune with me. I didn't even have to say anything. She always knew what was going on with me. We're very close. We have had special and close relationship, even though I had this kind of sister."

"My sister is really great. I talk about her a disgusting amount."

"I get excited talking about it. She does things I could never do and it amazes me we're blood related."

"When she feels good, is confident, she's like a tornado. She really tears it up, out there on the carpet. Everybody sits there in awe. Nobody can believe what she has done. When she finishes, there's a pause, then applause. When she's feeling it, she's unbelievable. I'm in awe of her."

"She's the only super-competitive one in our extended family. We're athletic but nobody took it to the level she did. It's amazing."

"I think she must have been a famous trapeze artist, or something like that, in a previous life."

"I've been the outsider, the objective observer, watching Alex and also my mom discover this sport and deal with everything in the world of rhythmic gymnastics. It's quite something."

"At first, I was disgusted. I'd be watching television with my little sister and she would sit there with her legs wrapped around her neck, or something, over stretching to get more flexible. Frankly, it was unnerving."

"For years, when we were younger, Alex was just my bratty little sister, going into my room, stealing things, breaking my toys, so I'd come home from school and yell at her, and that was our relationship."

"We are very different in a lot of superficial ways. The major difference is that I'm a chicken and I hate competition. However, we are a lot alike in important ways, such as the way we think. It's getting to be more so now. Her mannerisms are like mine, now, and I think that's cool. I hated it when she acted like me when she was a little kid. I thought she was mimicking me, making fun of me, even though mom said she was trying to be like me because she loved me so much."

"I did karate as a kid and I liked it a lot but it was on Saturday mornings and getting up to go was difficult so I dropped it after awhile. I was sad that I stopped. It was fun and it was something I could share with my dad. On weekends, in the back yard, I'd throw punches at him, we'd spar, and he'd pretend to punch me, but stop just short, scaring the heck out of my mother."

"I figure skated quite a bit and I did one competition but I got so nervous I thought I'd throw up. Alex is the opposite. She thrives on competition. She was so different, I thought she must be adopted. She was so crazy about sports and super-competitive, very driven, right from the start."

"I'm driven in my own way and Dad and Mom do things to their very best. They always told us, "Do your best", but Alex really took it to heart in an extreme way. My sister's best was always better than mine, especially in sports. I don't understand how she does what she does. In competitions, I'd freeze. I really didn't like being judged. Alex has always loved that."

"I get nauseous just watching her compete, I feel so nervous for her. When they say her name, announcing she's the next competitor, my heart beats fast. It breaks my heart, watching her, when she makes a mistake or when she does really well. If she drops the apparatus, I feel as though I've dropped it. It's as though I carry her nerves, the scary nerves. She doesn't get nervous. I used to think, "She's not human, she's a gymnast robot". But she's not robotic in the way some of the girls from the former Soviet Union are. Those girls are hardcore gymnast robots. They kind of freak me out. Alex and the other North American girls have an advantage over the Russians and some of the others. Our girls can live more balanced lives; it isn't all about gymnastics, which makes them more human, and it shows in the way they perform on the carpet."

"There is a four-year age difference between us so when I was a teenager she seemed quite a bit younger than me."

"I didn't know anything about rhythmic gymnastics, when she started. It was as though she was in this different world and I didn't know her anymore."

"She was traveling all the time or in the gym so we were hardly ever in the same house at the same time, growing up. I wouldn't even know her favourite colour, in those days, or any of the things you might expect sisters to know about each other."

"She's my little sister and I think of her that way except

when I go into her room and see all the medals. That room. Wow! It's not always easy to have a sister whose room is a trophy room. It's like dammit, where're my medals?! You walk in and there's a shelf with a bar underneath it, to hold up all the trophies, which are just stacked up on top of each other. So many medals hang from the bar but there isn't enough room for them in that room. There are medals in every room of the house. It's funny. You find them everywhere. Somebody asks to see one, or some of them, and they get left in the living room, or the kitchen. You're always finding a medal somewhere."

"Her room is a trophy room. I've wanted to build a trophy room so I could claim all those trophies as my own. I've got three medals: one for that one skating competition I went in, one for being the most improved basketball player when I was in Grade Eight, and one was an award for vocal music in Grade Eight. I got the most improved player in basketball because at the start of the season I tried to score on my own basket but then I learned which way to go."

High School Confidential

"I was in my high school choir. I went to an arts high school in Toronto called Cardinal Carter School for the Arts. I'd love to have a choir of elementary kids."

"When I went away to University, we became close, at last. Oddly enough, we got very close when I moved out of the house. When I was doing my own thing, and she was doing her own thing, we were able to come together. We'd call each other on the phone a lot and then we became best friends. I was 19 and she was 15."

"When she was younger, she had crushes on boys, but she didn't have the time to do anything about it. She definitely had crushes on the same guys as the rest of the girls at school. Guys liked her, too. When you're 16, it's hard to get to know somebody who's always in Bulgaria or Russia or someplace. Guys are in awe of her. She's hot. She's very good looking. My guy friends are all in love with her. When she came up to Queen's to visit me, she caused quite a commotion. She's hot stuff. I had to tell them to lay off because she was still a high school kid, only 18. She's never had anyone in her life that she was really serious about. She dates as much as she can. She'll go out with a guy she likes but it's hard for her to have anything serious. Her sport has to come first, in order for her to achieve her goals. Also, she's in University and that means she has a lot of schoolwork to do. She's traveling all the time. She's had boyfriends but it's always ended. Relationships take work. Guys are intimidated by her. She's a beautiful 19-year - old who has been around the world and who wins gold medals all the time. Guys want to impress girls and it's hard to impress someone who has done all that. Also, she's really really strong, and that can be intimidating for the average guy."

"When she's older, she'll probably find another athlete. She has some great guy friends. They had so much fun at the Commonwealth Games. Those guys could understand her because they share the same goals. They are all so driven."

"It's probably gotta be really hard for her. You want to have somebody to share experiences with, somebody who understands you, but nobody her age has been able to do that, so far."

"I was an English major at Queen's, interested in educational psychology, and now I'm taking a year off to volunteer in schools so next year I can start teacher training and become an elementary school teacher. I plan to teach primary school, to start, but I'd love to teach high school English later on."

"I've traveled to Vancouver and Edmonton to see Alex compete, and I wanted to go to Venezuela, Brazil, Hawaii, Australia, but her competitions happened at exam time. This year, I'll see her compete more, since I'm taking the year off."

"Thank God Alex went to Havergal. She had some pretty amazing people in her corner while she was there. Especially in her last year, she wasn't there much. I thought it would take her five years. They made her packages to take with her, got tutoring when she came back, changed exam schedules. Her guidance counselor was amazing, Miss Pinslor."

"Mary Sanders had a tough time in high school. She didn't get the same kind of support and had to do an extra half year. When she was away, she didn't get any extra help. Alex could go away for a month for competitions."

"It was fun to watch her in first year in University because she was out of her element. She'd call me hysterically, 'I was away for two weeks and this assignment is due.' She did disgustingly well. I tried to coach her through some of the rough parts, I wanted her to be a part-time student. She figured out how to do things better. She's mathematical and logical, analyzes things and figures out how to do them better. She never says, 'I can't'."

"Alex isn't normal, but outside of the gym, she becomes normal, again, very quickly, and blends right in. At movies, or parties, or when she comes out with me and my friends, she fits in and doesn't seem like a freaky gymnast robot at all. Unless somebody asks her about it, she doesn't even talk about what she does as an athlete. When she does talk about it, she's very humble about her accomplishments. She laughs if people tease her about being a rhythmic gymnast. Sometimes somebody will say something like, 'Hey Al, put your legs on your head,' or something."

Alex the Great at the 2006 Commonwealth Games

"Lots of people call her Alex. I call her Ali, or Squirt, or Seestor. I have a lot of names for her. But I've never heard anyone call her Alex the Great, except during the Commonwealth Games, after she won all the gold medals, and sportscasters picked up on it after it was in the newspapers in Australia."

"During the Commonwealth Games, I had all my friends on TV watch, checking for coverage. All my housemates at University were e-mailing me articles and pictures when they appeared online. We all went crazy on the last day of the Commonwealth Games because on the news they showed snippets of all her gold medal winning routines. I sat and cried with a friend from high school who was one of my housemates. It was very moving because of the way she performs and also because I knew how badly she wanted it."

To The Olympics

"The up-coming Olympics make me so nervous, I honestly don't know how I'm going to survive them. I get very nervous for nationals and even more nervous for the big international events. I know she'll do really well. The thing with her is they really like her internationally because she's very passionate, very European, not stiff, and she really captures the audience. She is also very artistic and technical."

"Under the pressure of Olympics, if she can do clean routines, she will be in the top 15 at least and that's an amazing accomplishment for a Canadian in Russian-and-Bulgarian-dominated sport."

The Story Of Alex And Mary

"The 2004 Olympic thing was so stressful. The whole thing with the USA and Mary seemed like one big political game. I'm happy my sister didn't go to the US, although I wanted her to go to the Olympics."

"It was Mary's time to go, but it wasn't the right time for Alex. Everybody has a time to go. Mary took it. She can now say she was an Olympian. I don't think Alex was ready to go. If it was the right moment and the right circumstances, she would have gone. The opportunity was there, but she didn't take it. She could have gone with the American team."

"I'm a little bit superstitious. I believe everything happens for a reason. You have to follow your gut. People are more in-tune with themselves than they realize. When you're ready for something like that, you just know. Alex just knows. She's always been able to predict a bit how she'll do in a competition, what scores she'll get in an event, to some extent."

"I felt really sick about the way things were handled at the time of the last Olympics. I was so angry. My sister was quiet, all that time. She went inside her own head. I was worried about her but didn't have to be. I couldn't tell what she was thinking. A lot of times I feel we're on the same wavelength but we weren't communicating at that time. I was so angry, I wanted to yell at somebody. I wanted everybody to know it was so unfair. First, they got her hopes up, said 'You're going, don't worry'. And then they took it all away. They shouldn't have made the promise in the first place. Nothing is guaranteed in life. And then to take it away .... She was so young. She hadn't faced that kind of injustice, before. She was young, she was new, she was fresh, and she was so hungry for it. They promised it to her and then took it all away. It was brutal."

"I wanted her to bounce back but I didn't know how she could. It depends on your personality. Anybody else would have said, 'This is unfair and I quit.' She won't quit after something like that. She'll go out only after the most amazing competition of her life. Then she'll be ready to put it down. She won't stop until then. I can see her doing it for the rest of her life. She loves it so much."

"Bouncing back after a disappointment the way she does is really something. It's an Alex thing. Train harder at a higher level. Other people get down after a loss. For her, that's a waste of time. She finds something in her routine she can do better. It's a coping mechanism so she doesn't get down. She uses that energy to do something productive. She's not a complete robot. She'll get upset. She'll cry, come off carpet, shake it off, and then say, what's next? It's kind of neurotic. It's all about improving, for her. In her career as an athlete, she has always been improving. Every time you see her, she's always a bit better. I don't see her all the time, so I see her progressing."

"It was a little weird when Mary was around a lot because Alex and I were doing our own things and then Alex had Mary. She was two years older than Alex and two years younger than me. Before that, I thought of my sister as the baby. She hung out with Mary and older friends, my age, and we started hanging out together. Alex was always the youngest. I never felt threatened by Mary. I was glad she was there for Alex because Mary understood the world of rhythmic gymnastics. They were inseparable. I knew her well, and got along with her well, but I stayed away from the gym and gymnastics in those days. I was involved in other things."

"Mary and Alex had a friend named Kelly and we became friends. Then I hung out with my little sister. We did a lot of things as a foursome. We used to go to Canada's Wonderland. Alex liked the big rides, especially the upside-down roller coasters. She went on all those rides about a year before me, and she was four years younger than me. As soon as she was old enough or big enough, as soon as they would let her on, she'd be right in there. She talked me into trying them and I just screamed. I had a fear of falling out. I was a worrywart as a kid, compared to Alex."

"The sport is kind of crazy because of the politics, which is like figure skating. There are many times at competitions when my mom says, 'Victoria, keep your comments to yourself'. I learned to be very good. I try not to get enraged by the scores or the judges. I still get upset with the way the sport is sometimes."

Just Alex?

"But what is Alex really like? Deep down, at heart, she's a goofball! She's so disciplined and mature for her age, but she's really goofy. The two of us can sit around and laugh like five-year-olds. That's what happens when it is just the two of us together. It's a weird sister thing. Maybe that's the reason we have the relationship we do, right now - we're making up for lost time."

Chapter 14. The Commonwealth Games Record-Setting Six Gold Medals

Television coverage and international headlines told the world the story: "Orlando wins 6 gold at Games", "Orlando golden", "Alex the Great Set Commonwealth Record".

Alexandra Orlando was well ahead of the competition, seizing the gold with a total score of 54.625 points. She scored 13.575 for ball, 13.425 for clubs, 13.225 for ribbon, and 14.400 for rope, for the highest apparatus score of the competition.

She was surprised with some of her performances, despite her dominance in the competition.

Rope was her best routine, but it's usually her worst apparatus, so she was pretty happy with that, but she was disappointed with her qualifying-day clubs routine, because she dropped them.

She very rarely drops her clubs or any apparatus. The performance was very unusual for her. Despite that mistake, the rest of her routine was flawless.

Alex also won the gold in the Team Final.

Durratun Nashihin Rosli of Malaysia finished in second place with scores of 13.275 for rope, 12.925 for ball, 12.950 for clubs, 11.675 for ribbon and an All-around score of 50.825.

Canadian Yana Tskiaridze won the bronze with scores of 12.375 for rope, 11.575 for ball, 12.875 for clubs, 12.750 for ribbon and an All-around score of 49.575.

At the previous Commonwealth Games, in Kuala

Lumpur, Thye Chee Kiat's high scoring led Malaysia to an upset victory over defending champion Canada in the rhythmic gymnastics team competition. Thye helped the Malaysians edge ahead 93.023 to 92.962 at the end with a 9.500 in her last routine, with the clubs. Australia won the bronze with 92.937.

Canada's Erika-Leigh Stirton had the only marks higher than Thye's with a 9.600 for the clubs and 9.500's for the hoop and ribbon. Se had 9.450 for the rope. Thye had a 9.475 for each the rope and hoop, and 9.200 for the ribbon, helping a powerful advance by a team that had finished last at the 1994 games.

Shaneez Paulston of Australia won silver in the clubs and ribbon, with Canadian Emilie Livingston and Malaysian Carolyn Au-Yong the respective bronze medallists.

"She wasn't the most sparkly or even the most flexible rhythmic gymnast to come to Melbourne, but Alexandra Orlando was by far the best."

Alex set high goals for herself at the Melbourne Commonwealth Games. She believed she could win five gold medals. She won all six. The previous Commonwealth record was five gold medals by Canada's Erika-Leigh Stirton at the 1998 Games.

Rhythmic Gymnastics Team Competition Final Results:

1. Canada	128,775
2. Malaysia	124,175
3. Australia	117,175
4. England	108,400
5. South Africa	106,075
6. Cyprus	104,150

"The greatest moment was seeing that Canadian flag fly when Alex was on the podium," Marisa Orlando says. "We had a great time in Melbourne."

She tells the story like a veteran at colour commentary. "At the Commonwealth Games in Australia, the Malaysian team was very close to the Canadian team and it was thrilling to see the competition unfold. At the final flag raising, after Alex's 12th routine, she waved goodbye to the crowd, and it was quite a moment because the results hadn't been announced but everybody in that huge crowd just knew she had won another gold."

"The euphoria was rising and we were all crying. And then they announced the record - six gold medals at the Commonwealth Games - and ten thousand people all cheered! They were all so involved in the moment. It was amazing."

The motto of the Commonwealth Games in Melbourne was 'united in the moment'. Everyone involved in those Games was certainly united at that moment when it was announced an athlete had won a record number of gold medals.

"It was exciting to see Alex on the Jumbotron, with all six gold medals," her mother reports. "Alex got a lot of attention in Australia and wherever she went after that. Her picture was in all the papers and people were always asking her for her autograph. It has been nice for her."

The Orlandos were impressed with the way Australia handled the 2006 Commonwealth Games and with the Australian approach to sports in general.

"Australia gets the right coaches, builds terrific venues, and has amazing support from the people," Marisa Orlando says. "Their volunteers all wore blue shirts and you saw them everywhere. If you were in the subway, or wherever, and you needed help, you just asked someone wearing a blue shirt. They were friendly and so much help. The whole city was buzzing. It was so much fun. It was like the Olympics, only friendlier, they say."

At the 18th Commonwealth Games in Melbourne, Australia, there were 71 countries participating, with 4,500 athletes in 16 sports with 247 events. The Games were opened by Queen Elizabeth II. Both the Melbourne Cricket Ground and the Yarra River were centrepieces for the Opening Ceremony, which included a lot of fireworks, watched by Queen Elizabeth II in her capacity as Head of the Commonwealth. The Games proved to be the largest sporting event ever staged in Melbourne, eclipsing the 1956 Summer Olympics in terms of the number of teams competing, athletes competing, and events being held.

The site for the opening and closing ceremonies was the Melbourne Cricket Ground, which was also used during Melbourne's 1956 Olympic Games. The mascot for the games was Karak, a Red-tailed Black Cockatoo, a threatened species.

The change from daylight savings time to standard time in Australian states that follow was pushed back from March 26 to April 2 for 2006 to avoid affecting the games. In order to deal with the change, software company and official technology partner of the Games, Microsoft released a daylight savings patch for their Windows line of operating systems.

CBC, CBC Newsworld, and CBC Country Canada aired daily one-hour highlights show of the Commonwealth Games back home in Canada.

On day 11 of the Commonwealth Games Canadian rhythmic gymnast Alexandra Orlando won four gold medals, tying a record with six gold medals overall. The 19-year-old from Toronto was named Canada's flag-bearer for the closing ceremony. Orlando tied a record first set 28 years ago by Canadian swimmer, Graham Smith, at the Commonwealth Games in Edmonton. Two Australian swimmers have equaled it since - Susie O'Neill in Kuala Lumpur in 1998 and Ian Thorpe in Manchester, England, four years later. Orlando completed the rhythmic gymnastics competition having won six gold medals - a gold in every rhythmic gymnastics event - to become only the fourth competitor to win six gold medals at a single Commonwealth Games.

Unlike most other competitors, Alex's music, choreography and costume design reflected maturity, athleticism, and energy. Orlando dressed in a black netted number with green crystal detailing. She went for demure and classic rather than the glitz and glamour.

Her first gold was in the Team Final, where Canada out-classed their nearest rivals Malaysia and Australia. The Canadian team of Alexandra Orlando, Yana Tsikaridze and Carly Orava scored 128.775 points, ahead of silver medallists Malaysia, 124.175, and the home team, 117.175.

Alex progressed to the Individual All-around Final where she scored 14.400 for Rope, 13.575 for Ball, 13.725 for Clubs and 12.950 for Ribbon. Her All-around total of 54.325 improved on her score of 52.650, which secured her 18th place at the 2005 World Championships.

Orlando left her main rivals in her wake, with Malaysian Durratun Nashihin Rosli picking up the silver 50.825 and Tsikaridze bronze 49.575.

She posted world-class scores. With a difficulty of 5.950 in her ball routine, the judges awarded her 8.300 for execution and 7.150 for artistic elements. Her clubs were impeccable, despite Orlando admitting to a few nerves after dropping the apparatus in the All-around Final. With the highest difficulty in the competition, she scored 14.200. Orlando completed her haul with 13.775 in the ribbon.

Orlando's six gold medals were an important addition to a Canadian team that recorded scores of personal bests and dozen of Canadian and Commonwealth Games' records. Canada's 253 athletes won 86 medals (26 gold, 29 silver, 31 bronze) over the course of the 11 days of competition. Canada achieved its goal of finishing in the top three countries overall.

The final medal count, for the gold, silver, and bronze at the 2006 Commonwealth Games was:

1. Australia: 84 gold, 69 silver, 68 bronze = 221 total
2. England: 36 gold, 40 silver, 34 bronze = 110 total
3. Canada: 26 gold, 29 silver, 31 bronze =   86 total

The next Commonwealth Games will be held in Delhi, India, in 2010. Canada is bidding to host the Games in 2014 in Halifax.

The great results from these Games, following on the heels of a record-setting performance at the Olympic Winter Games in Torino, are further evidence that Canada is an emerging power on the international sport scene in both summer and winter sports.

Good news for rhythmic gymnastics in Canada: Alexandra Orlando figures she'll hang around a while longer in the sport she so thoroughly dominated at the 18th Commonwealth Games.

"I don't think I'm ever, ever going to take them (her six gold medals) off," Orlando said. "I have to say, I really like them. They could become my new accessory."

It was a sweet moment at the end of a brilliant week for Orlando, who was bitterly disappointed after being denied the opportunity to compete at the 2004 Summer Olympics in Athens.

Her father says, "What Alex did at Melbourne is unbelievable. But I expected it. I knew she had it in her. She has the drive and the ambition. But anything could happen. I knew she could do it."

Reporters asked her the inevitable question: How does it feel? She simply told them it was overwhelming.

Chapter 15: After The Gold

The rave reviews Alexandra received via the headlines of newspapers around the world did not stop at the end of the Commonwealth Games. Shortly after her return to Canada, the Vancouver newspaper headlines announced "Commonwealth Games star Alexandra Orlando continued her winning ways by capturing the All-around title at the Canadian rhythmic gymnastics championships in Surrey, BC." and "Orlando golden at rhythmic gymnastics nationals".

After the Commonwealth Games in Australia, Alex got a good deal of recognition. The Mayor of Toronto invited her to a council meeting and stopped proceedings to give her some attention as an athlete from Toronto who won world-wide recognition. She has been invited to banquets to speak and was invited to Puerto Rico to demonstrate her sport, not just to compete. She is getting a good deal of attention internationally, if not so much at home.

Newspapers referred to her as "Commonwealth Games star Alexandra Orlando". The headlines in Vancouver said, "Orlando Set To Defend Rhythmic Gymnastics Title".

There is certainly some pressure when you are the defending champion, returning home from an international event, and expected to win, Alexandra discovered after she announced she would compete up until the 2008 Olympics. She said she would try to not let the pressure get to her and enjoy the event. Her personal goal, she claimed, was to improve her rope routine, which was not her strongest.

Orlando's top challengers at Canadian Nationals were expected to be Commonwealth Games teammates Yana Tsikaridze, of Montreal, Carly Orava, Stefanie Carver, and Rachel Cossar, of Toronto. The Canadian championships were the second and final selection event to determine the national team for the season. The Elite Canada competition counted for 35 percent towards selection.

She followed up her Commonwealth Games performance by capturing the national senior All-around title at the Canadian rhythmic gymnastics championships in Surrey, BC. She scored top marks in all disciplines, including ball and rope as well as clubs and ribbon, and finished the championship with 59.150 points out of a possible 80.

Carly Orava, also of Toronto, placed 2nd with 55.175 points, while Montreal's Yana Tsikaridze was 3rd at 54.100.

The victory gave Orlando her 4th National All-around title.

Just before the Commonwealth Games, Alexandra posted four victories in the Elite Canada competitions, which was also the Commonwealth Games selection trials. She won in rope at 14.575 points, clubs at 14.175 and ball at 15.000, after picking up the All-around win.

Montreal's Yana Tsikaridze denied Orlando a golden sweep, winning the ribbon competition at 15.025.

After leading Canada's athletes into the closing ceremonies of the Commonwealth Games in Australia, Alex started to shift her focus to qualifying for the 2008 Olympic Games in Beijing.

Before the Commonwealth Games, her best international result came at the 2005 world championships, where she placed 18th overall in the individual All-around competition.

She told reporters she would like to finish in the top 15

at one of her international events coming up this year, but she knows she'll have tougher competition than she faced in Melbourne.

Eastern European countries like Russia, Ukraine, Belarus, Bulgaria, Azerbaijan and Kazakhstan tend to dominate rhythmic gymnastics.

A few months after returning home from the Commonwealth Games with all those gold medals, Alexandra was still reeling from the once-in-a lifetime experience.

Her life got hectic after the Commonwealth Games, with national championships and lots of requests for interviews, followed by final examinations at the University of Toronto. She was the subject of articles in The Globe and Mail, Toronto Star, and North York Mirror, among others. She was also interviewed by news anchor Diana Swain for a segment that appeared on the *CBC's News at Six*. She said it took a while for her victory in Australia to sink in.

She confessed to one reporter that there was so much going on in her life, it was hard to keep track of it all. She said it was "kind of crazy". After a decade of winning championships without getting much recognition in Canada, it was hard for her to get used to being in the paper and on TV.

She returned to her life as a first-year Commerce student at the University of Toronto, but started making plans to put her studies on hold while trying to earn a berth at the 2008 Olympics in Beijing.

Alex decided to put her focus on next year's Olympic trials, and not attempt to combine 25-hours-a-week in the gym with the demands of University life.

It was a huge decision, she says, and she had to really look inside herself. She wanted to be sure she was doing it for the right reasons. For Alex, the reasons for extending her career were compelling but she wanted to be certain she was still competing for herself. Since the time she started rhythmic gymnastics, she dreamed of competing at the Olympic Games, but now that she was 19, she had to think about it again.

In 2004, she had almost reached her goal of making it to the Olympics. She qualified as an alternate for the Olympic Games in Athens. But then there was the controversy and the conflict. She did not want to go through anything like that again.

She thought about quitting the sport, briefly, but decided to train harder and crack the top ten or 15 in the world, instead.

Chapter 16. To The Olympics -- And Beyond!

"I've had the Olympic dream since I was seven," Alex says "And I came close to getting there the last time so I am motivated for the next Olympics."

Her mother says, "I hope the Canadian federation and the whole country will be behind Alex and the Canadian team at the next Olympics. They deserve it."

"As for the next Olympics, I never thought we would be talking about that," Paul Orlando says. "I thought Alex would quit when she was 16-years-old and had that huge disappointment over the last Olympics. But then she placed 16 out of 150 at the worlds and decided to go on."

He remains supportive but not overzealous about Alex's results.

"If she gets the chance to go to the Olympics, she's gonna work hard, train hard," her father adds. "I don't know about medals. It's possible. Could it actually happen?"

"If Alex gets there, and I believe she will, I'm certain she will be inspired to turn in the best performance of her life - and that's really saying something," Lori Fung says. "If that happens, who knows about the standings or medals."

Representatives of the Canadian Olympic Committee went to Rio de Janeiro well in advance of the Pan American Games Rio 2007.

Betty Dermer-Norris, the COC director who is responsible for the planning of the Canadian delegations, reported that her country should send to the Games a delegation of about 425 athletes and approximately 700 people in the whole.

"This will be the second largest Canadian delegation sent to Pan American Games, smaller just than the delegation sent to Winnipeg-1999, in Canada itself. It is also larger than our delegation in Athens", Betty Dermer-Norris explained.

COC Project Manager commented that by taking part in RIO 2007, the Canadian athletes will prepare for the Olympic Games Beijing-2008.

"We will bring our best athletes in all the disciplines that will qualify for Beijing-2008", added Project Manager Carla Anderson.

The Canadian representatives have already met with the key areas of the Organizing Committee of the XV Pan American Games Rio 2007 to discuss the progress of the organization of the multi-sport event and specific aspects of the operation and logistics of the Canadian delegation.

They also visited the venues that will be used at Games time and were able to observe the progress of the works. "This partnership with the National Olympic Committees is critical to the success of the Games. Thanks to their comments we can continuously improve our work", says Ana Mariza Ribeiro, the General Manager of International Relations.

Other members of the Canadian delegation are the Manager of the High Yield Program of the Canadian Cycling Association, Sean O'Donnell, and two representatives from Sports Canada, a Canadian government agency responsible for the development of sport in the country.

Rebeccah Bornemann and Serge de Blois are planning to directly involve the Canadian community in Brazil in the Games. "The objective is to have them taking part as volunteers in activities such as the distribution of uniforms to athletes at the Pan American Village", Rebeccah explained.

Thanks to the COC, Alexandra is now a 'carded' athlete, which means she gets financial support from the government to help with her expenses as an athlete competing for Canada at international events.

"Carding pays for training, competition suits, and travel, on a monthly basis," Marisa Orlando explains. "Gymnastics Canada pays for the major competitions. Nobody pays for training camps so we still have to cover that. There are very good camps in Bulgaria, Russia, and France. Also, we wanted to bring over a choreographer from Bulgaria to give us a different point of view. We invited Maria Petrova because she is the reigning champion of rhythmic gymnastics and she loves Alex."

Gymnastics Canada

Gymnastics Canada is the national governing body for the sport of gymnastics in Canada. First established in 1969, Gymnastics Canada works closely with the Provincial/Territorial Organizations and the 700+ local clubs to provide a broad range of programs and services to meet the needs of all participants. In addition, Gymnastics Canada represents our gymnastic community internationally at the Federation Internationale de Gymnastique (FIG), as well as domestically with the Canadian Olympic Committee and Commonwealth Games Canada.

Gymnastics Canada sets the operating standards and practices for the sport in Canada, from athlete development and coaching education, to judging certification.

The affairs of the Federation are under the direction of the Board of Directors. The GCG Board of Directors sets and evaluates the policies of the Federation. The Professional staff, with the assistance of the volunteer committees, lead, develop, implement, and manage programs and services according to the policies.

The main goal for Gymnastics Canada right now is to qualify Canadian athletes for the 2008 Olympics.

Their objective is to identify our potential Olympic Group; create a new category 'Olympic Development Group', which will be under the auspices of the NTAC; facilitate a headstart of the preparation towards 2008; develop a long-term program to enable our Canadian Group athletes to achieve performance excellence at the world level; guide the multi-year group training program to enable athletes to achieve the ceiling of their potential; and seek financial support to carry out the preparation for the 2004 - 2008 cycle.

The strategy of Gymnastics Canada, starting in 2007, is to achieve consistent world class performance at the most prestigious competitions throughout the year; rank among the top ten countries at the World Championships or be the top-ranked country from the Americas and qualify Canada for the 2008 Olympic Games; fully fund the National Team Group to the World Championships, two strategic events, and a three-week camp in Europe; build international experience and reputation; fully fund the NT Group to at least one strategic competition; partially fund it to at least two strategic competitions and a camp in Europe; maintain the image of Canada being a top contender for Olympic participation; send a group only if able to fulfill the Group Performance Criteria at World Level; encourage competition between the existing groups; and facilitate the strive for excellence.

"Gymnastics Canada has been so supportive," Alex says. "When I retire from my sport, after the Olympics, I'd like to do something for them. I've got so much support from them. They're always checking in to see if I'm okay, happy, and so on. They're a huge part of my support system."

The Competition

For Alexandra Orlando, the Commonwealth Games in Australia were the beginning of a long road to qualifying for the 2008 Beijing Olympics.

After dominating the Commonwealth Games, she told reporters she would like to finish in the top 15 in international events, but she knew she would have tougher competition than she faced in Melbourne. Eastern European countries like Russia, Ukraine, Belarus, Bulgaria, Azerbaijan, and Kazakhstan tend to dominate rhythmic gymnastics.

One of Alex's main competitors has been, and will continue to be, Cynthia Valdez, according to Marisa Orlando. "Cynthia, from Mexico, trains in Moscow," she says. "I like Cynthia. Alex and Cynthia have always been close, in terms of competitions. They flip back and forth, but Alex is usually ahead by a few points. Cynthia has been training in Europe full-time for the past three years and it has not changed her results enormously. She hasn't been home for a long time."

"They go to lots of little competitions," Paul Orlando points out. "That's why the Europeans are way ahead of the North Americans. There is always a competition to go to in Bulgaria or Spain or somewhere. The athletes are like professionals - they really get paid to train and compete in their sport. Also, the sport is more popular there and has been for a long time."

The Russians

"It's hard to beat the Russians," Paul Orlando says. "They're machines! Their athletes don't live at home, they live in sports compounds, and they train seven days a week. Alex has a life. She trains hard, but not eight hours a day."

In 2004, at the Olympic Games in Athens, Greece, the Russians had to jump through hoops, as they say, to win a gold medal. The defending Olympic champions won another gold in group rhythmic gymnastics, scoring 51.100 points to edge Italy and Bulgaria in the colourful smorgasbord of tossing and twirling. Eight teams of five women each vied for the championship. Each had two turns on the mat - one with five ribbons, the other with three hoops and two balls.

The Russians also won a bronze in 1996, the year group rhythmic was added to the games. Italy won its first Olympic medal in the sport. Bulgaria, which won silver at the Atlanta Olympics, returned to the medal stand after being shut out in 2000.

Sports in Russia is something that seems more important to people than politics, the economy, or the weather. In the Soviet era, athletics were promoted as an important part of life for everyone. Russia has been changing at a dizzying pace. For decades, it was the heart of the Union of Soviet Socialist Republics, or the USSR, or the CCCP, in their Cyrillic alphabet. The Soviet Union was a communist empire. The communist and Soviet rule collapsed in the early 1990s. Russia, also known as the Russian Federation, was still a big, powerful, country.

The break-up of the Soviet Union fractured its sports programs, which had been world beaters, in some regards. The Soviet constitution had physical fitness written right into it. To be a strong people, the people had to be physically-fit, they believed. The people loved sports.

The communists ruled for over 70 years and came close to war with the other superpower, the United States of

America, during the Cold War. In the 1980s, communism declined, the Soviet Union began to crumble, and many of the communist governments in Eastern European countries were overthrown.

In 1991, the Soviet Union came to an end. The 15 republics that had been part of the USSR or CCCP became independent nations. Together they were called the Commonwealth of Independent States, or the CIS.

Ice hockey is the national sport in Russia, as it is in Canada. Soccer is the most popular sport, in terms of fan appeal, in the former Soviet Union.

During the Cold War, the Soviet controlled countries and the democracies of the West used the Olympics as the primary arena for their rivalry. Each Olympic medal was seen as a political triumph as well as an athletic victory, especially by the USSR. Athletes representing the USSR were incredibly well-trained.

After the break up of the USSR, the countries of the former USSR participated under the name of the Unified Team, for the 1992 Olympics. Then, beginning with the 1994 Olympics, the former countries competed as independent nations.

"Sometimes I wish there was just one big communist country, as in the days of the USSR, as it would cut down on the competition, particularly in rhythmic gymnastics," Marisa Orlando says.

The USA boycotted the 1980 Olympics in Moscow and the Soviets boycotted the Olympics in Los Angeles, USA in 1984.

Under the Soviet system, children with special athletic talents were searched for, discovered, and enrolled in special sports schools. They left home at very early ages. At one time, there were more than five thousand sports schools across the USSR. Many of those schools still exist. They produced generations of champions, including gymnasts.

Larissa Latynina won a record 18 Olympic medals, including nine gold, between 1956 and 1964.

Olga Korbut remains the all-time darling of Soviet gymnastics. In the 50s and the 60s, Soviet athletes were seen as cold and technical, performing almost like machines in a factory. Olga Korbut had a lively personality to go with her flawless technique.

Nadia Comaneci, from Romania, captivated the hearts of millions of television viewers at the 1976 Olympics in Montreal with her perfect scores in seven events and won five Olympic medals. She was also the first Romanian in history to win an Olympic gymnastic gold medal.

Comaneci's coach, Bela Karolyi, defected from Romania to the USA and he coached Mary Lou Retton to gold at the 1984 Olympic Games in L.A, as the first American gymnast ever to win the overall title.

The 1984 Olympic Games were not boycotted by the East, they said, but 17 countries did not compete and they called it a non-participation. Those countries had won almost 60 percent of the gold medals at the Montreal Olympics. Russia led the non-participation, and blamed it on anti-communist demonstrations in the USA, saying the safety of their athletes could not be guaranteed. Bulgaria, Cuba, Poland, Czechoslovakia and East Germany all followed Russia's lead.

Russia defended its title in team rhythmic gymnastics, at the last Olympic Games. The Russian team has won medals in event in last three Olympics. The Russians also won a bronze in 1996, the year group rhythmic was added to the games.

Italy won its first Olympic medal in the sport. Bulgaria, which won silver at the Atlanta Olympics, returned to the medal stand after being shut out in 2000 final results

Would Alex benefit from one on one coaching, the way the Russians do it?

"I think it's a question of backing," Paul Orlando says "The Russians have millions dollars and amazing complexes dedicated to the sport, staffed with coaches, doctors, physiotherapists, sports psychologists, 24/7. Canada doesn't have the facilities. Alex's gym is good but it can't even compare with the facilities built by some other countries. The Russians train for the qualifying events in Olympic facilities."

China

In China, traditional sports stress individual perfection and aim at balancing the yin and yang for health and longevity. Artistry, form, and balance are all goals of these sports, as they are with rhythmic gymnastics.

Kung fu comes from China. Acrobatics is also enormously important to the history of China. Acrobatics stresses balance, grace, flexibility, and strength, as does rhythmic gymnastics. Chinese athletes have built on their traditional acrobatics to produce amazing male and female gymnasts.

Rhythmic gymnastics is a sport that is on the rise in China, as it is in Japan, and fabulous facilities have been created for the sport.

The USA

"The Americans push their way through to the worlds," Alex's father, Paul Orlando, says. "That's the way they are. Would it benefit Canadians to have that kind of drive? Absolutely. I can tend to be pushy. But I'm American and Alexandra is very Canadian. Most Canadians don't have the nationalism Alex has. Americans stand together. Canadians don't seem to have that. Does that attitude make them better? I don't think so. Maybe they need to do that to give themselves more confidence. But they come off as people who enjoy having all that attitude."

"In rhythmic gymnastics, we have a good attitude and wear the maple leaf proudly," Alex says. "That American attitude may work for the American athletes when they are at home, but I don't see it working for them when they are abroad. In rhythmic gymnastics, the Canadian and American teams get along very well and I would love to think that Mary and I had something to do with that. Before Mary went to the USA, our teams never spoke to each other and we had a lot of tension between us. I think that, no matter what sport it is, Canada and the US have this unspoken but serious rivalry."

Alex's Chances At The Olympics

"Alex has a chance to go to the 2008 Olympics, if it's all fair, and the COC stays away from their old policy of sending only the athletes in the top 12 internationally in their sport," Marisa Orlando, says.

"We used to send 40 athletes to the Olympics. She is going for it. The COC doesn't have that silly rule any more about sending only the top 12 in the world to the Olympics. If Alex goes to China, we're all going - her mom, dad, and sister, Victoria. I'm in Canada as much as the USA, now and I will have Canadian citizenship before the time of the next Olympic Games. She is taking two courses at the University of Toronto, instead of a full load, and she will train twice a day."

Alex's mother believes Alex does best at the highest levels of competition.

"When there are only 30 competitors, Alex really shines," she says. "At events where only two per country are allowed to compete, the odds are better for Alex."

"I believe the last Games was the first time Canada was not represented at the Olympics in rhythmic gymnastics," Marisa Orlando said, "so we might have to prove ourselves again. We have had such amazing gymnasts in the past years, and now a new younger set will begin. It might take a little time to build up our position again."

The Canadian Olympic Committee

The Canadian Olympic Committee is a national, private, not-for-profit organization committed to sport excellence. It is responsible for all aspects of Canada's involvement in the Olympic movement, including Canada's participation in the Olympic and Pan American Games and a wide variety of programs that promote the Olympic Movement in Canada through cultural and educational means.

In an effort to increase podium results at the 2008 and 2012 Olympic Games, the Canadian Olympic Committee released the Road to Excellence Business Plan, which sets the vision and strategy for Canada to improve its performance at the upcoming Games. The plan targets a top 16 placing for Canada at the 2008 Olympic Games in Beijing and a top 12 placing at the 2012 Olympic Games in London.

The goal for the 2008 and 2012 Paralympic Games is for Canada to place amongst the top five nations at each event. Similar to the Own the Podium 2010 winter sport initiative, the Road to Excellence plan targets sports with the ability to achieve success at upcoming Olympic and Paralympic Games.

"In many sports, the difference between finishing first and fourth usually comes down to a few one-hundredths of a second," said Anne Merklinger, Director General of Canoe Kayak Canada and member of the Summer Sport Steering Committee, which guided the plan's development. "The Road to Excellence Business Plan provides Canada's summer sport federations with an overview on how we can close and eliminate this gap in order to help us achieve greater podium success over the next six years."

Iain Brambell, a two-time Olympian in rowing and chair of the COC's Athletes' Council, says, "I'm very optimistic about the future of Canadian summer sport after seeing the Road to Excellence Business Plan. We've seen the success Canada's winter Olympians and Paralympians had in Turin and certainly this program has the potential to help more summer athletes reach the podium in both 2008 and 2012."

The business plan, authored by Dr. Roger Jackson, CEO of Own the Podium 2010 and a gold medallist in rowing at the 1964 Olympic Games, was developed with the input of Canadian and international sport experts, with a view toward establishing a more coordinated and effective Canadian sport system to better support athletes. The plan is also devised to build effective partnerships with governments, sports and associated organizations, delivering world-class programs, policies and financing. The plan outlines the need to generate additional federal and corporate funding of $58.8 million annually to support high performance programs for Olympic and Paralympic targeted summer sports. It also identifies an additional $29.6 million of annual support from provincial sources to augment junior and senior national athlete development, with the overall goal being to ensure sustainable funding up to and beyond 2012.

"The landscape of international high-performance sport is evolving at an aggressive rate," said CPC Chief

Operating Officer Brian MacPherson. "Countries from around the world are using every advantage at their disposal in order to provide their athletes with the ideal training environment. The Road to Excellence Business Plan will help Canada increase its number of medallists while also ensuring that those athletes continue to have access to the very best training resources available."

COC Chief Executive Officer Chris Rudge says, "With the initial success of the Own The Podium 2010 initiative, I am confident in the sport community's ability to develop and execute a similar initiative to help Canada's summer athletes and coaches reach the podium. The Road to Excellence Business Plan provides a blueprint for how we can provide Canadian summer sport athletes with the essential tools and resources necessary to achieve success."

The development of the Road to Excellence Business Plan marks the first time Canada's summer sport organizations have come together with their sport partners to map out a comprehensive plan for podium success. The plan would give Canadian athletes the required financial and technical support to help them be competitive at the highest level in preparation for the 2008 and 2012 Olympic Games.

BEIJING 2008: Games of the XXIX Olympiad

In order for Canadian athletes to qualify for the 2008 Canadian Olympic team, they must meet the qualification standards set by both the International Federation and National Sports Federation of their respective sport.

The International Gymnastics Federation has plans for the 29th Olympic Games in Beijing, China, in 2008 that include rhythmic gymnastics events for women, including individual competition and the group competition. They will have a quota of 96 women athletes for rhythmic gymnastics, including 24 for individual competition plus 12 groups of six for group competitions.

Qualification is based on the results of the 2007 World Championships. Places are allocated to National Olympic Committees and not to the gymnasts, with the exception of places 21 to 24 (individual) and 11 to 12 (group).

Places are allocated to the 12 best gymnasts of Competition II at the 2007 World Championships. Places are also allocated to the eight best gymnasts ranked 13 and lower in Competition II at the 2007 World Championships. Places 21 -23, known as the three "final qualification places" are granted by the FIG Executive Committee in agreement with the Technical Committee for Rhythmic Gymnastics. Those three spots are awarded to ensure that the host country of the Olympic Games is represented by at least one gymnast and to ensure all continents are represented.

If the host country, China, is not represented in places one to 20, one representative will be selected on the condition that she has participated in the 2007 World Championships. The place will be given to the best ranked gymnast from China in the 2007 World Championships. If gymnasts have to be selected to ensure all continents are represented at the Olympic Games, they will be given to the best ranked gymnast in the All-around competition from the continent in question at the 2007 World Championships.

All places which are not granted according to the criteria above will be granted according to the same criteria as applicable to places 13 to 20, in order to increase the number of gymnasts from countries not represented at the Olympic Games.

Qualification Timeline

The 2007 World Championships will take place in Patras, Greece, in September of 2007. By April of 2008, FIG will confirm the final allocation of places.

After The Olympics

"Alex is great with people and her sport had a lot to do with that," Paul Orlando says. "After she retires, if she goes into business, or whatever line of work, it will benefit, because of her experience. She knows how to work with people and she is very comfortable with crowds."

"After the Olympics, Alex will be at the top," her mother says. "I hope she will do some coaching but I think she will only do that on the side. She's very smart. She did well in first year of Commerce at the University of Toronto. In her second year, she's taking time off school to concentrate on her preparation for the Olympics. But she wants to study and get another profession and I'm sure she'll do well at whatever she chooses after this."

Future

"In the future, I'm certain that no matter what Alex does, she will be successful, because she has so much drive, determination, and discipline," Marisa Orlando says.

Victoria has her own ideas on the subject. "Alex is multi-talented," she says. "She's an amazing writer, too, but she doesn't have time to write. She wants to be a soccer player so badly. Soccer's the one sport I'm terrible at. I can't kick the ball. Alex likes volleyball, too. She plays beach volleyball. And she loves to sing. I secretly sort of think she'd be perfect in a movie about a dancer. I'd love to see her bust into acting. I can see her doing music videos. She's also an amazing choreographer. She does lots of collaboration on choreography with her coach."

When Alex met with the Mayor of Toronto, to be honoured by the City, he said, "Whatever you do in the future, do it in front of people, because you have fabulous presence." Marisa says.

"After the Olympics, there will be more schooling, for me," Alex says. "I would love to stay involved in Canadian sports, perhaps working with the Canadian Olympic Committee. Working in marketing and advertising also appeals to me. Athletes are a good fit for companies that make athletic products, such as running shoes, because athletes have lived through so much that's related to the company and their products. I want to be involved with Canadian athletes. I hope the younger girls start to rise, real soon, in rhythmic gymnastics. It's great to see younger people excelling in this sport in Canada. For coaching, in the future, I'm not sure about making a career of it, but I am coaching right now. I coach five-year-olds and it's very rewarding to see them improve. I love their energy and enthusiasm. They look so cute. And they make real progress real fast."

She says she loves traveling, even though she was getting a little tired of living out of a suitcase. "After studying abroad for year, then graduating, I'd like to live for a few years in lots of places, to get to know those places, instead of just passing through on my way to a competition," she says. "I love Europe, but miss home, while I'm there. I've traveled to France a dozen times, and I've been to Germany, England, Portugal, Spain, Bulgaria, Russia, Ukraine, Azerbaijan..... and Australia. I'd love to see all those places again, for longer periods of time than at a rhythmic gymnastics competition!"

New Sport

There is also the chance Alexandra Orlando will get involved in a relatively new sport.

"We are developing a new sport, called Aesthetic Group Gymnastics, which is like rhythmic gymnastics but is done with a group and there is no apparatus used," Annely Riga says. "There are lots of jumps and turns, based on rhythmic gymnastics moves. There are body waves, swings, and beautiful choreography. It's very good for the older girls and for women."

She adds, "I've been on the board for the International Federation of Aesthetic Group Gymnastics and a Chairperson of Promotion Committee for two years. Rhythmic gymnastics athletes can move into it as they get older. In 2008, Canada will host the world championships. The last one was in Finland. This will be the first time it is held in Canada. It will be in Toronto and we hope it will promote this new sport in Canada."

Chapter 17. Secrets Of Success And A Few Words Of Advice

Top Twelve Secrets Of Success

1. The Alexandra Orlando support system. Standing behind Alex, all the way, are her mother and father, her sister, her coach, and her club. "My parents, in particular, have helped me so much," she says.
2. The Coach: Dimitritchka "Mimi" Masleva. "My coach is great and our relationship just gets better as I get older."
3. Desire. "I want to be on the podium," Alex says.
4. Love of competition. "I love competing," she says. "I do it for myself and to have a good time, primarily."
5. Sportsmanship. "Years of competition and training, watching my teammates, getting their consolation, has taught me so much about sportsmanship."
6. Training hard. "I've always trained with older girls, at a higher level, and put in lots of hours."
7. Ritmika Rhythmic Gymnastics Club. "The support of my club is fantastic," she says. "They fundraise so I can travel. That blows my mind."
8. The team. " My teammates are all very close and that's a great support system."
9. Sacrifice. "Things like pizza, pasta, boyfriends, a lot of socializing, had to be sacrificed to be successful at this level," she says.
10. Competition. "Going to lots of competitions around the word and facing a lot of strong competition has helped."

11. Prioritizing. "My main priority is training and that's the way I want it to be."
12. Sisters. "My sister and friends I can talk to about everything without being judged."

"There is no secret to success in this sport," Marisa Orlando says. "Confidence does play a large part. It's very important to remain calm and collected, to refrain from getting flustered, at the big events. Training camps help with that. The opportunity to train with excellent athletes, world-class competitors, takes some of that edge off. It helped Alex a great deal with her confidence and her ability to remain calm at the big competitions."

Advice

Alexandra Orlando is a great public speaker, too, and is happy to talk to groups of young people, especially athletes.

"I feel funny about giving advice to students and young athletes because I'm still a student," Alex says. "As for high school - I was just there."

She believes young people relate better to people closer to her own age.

"My main advice is do not let anything get in the way, including friends and peer pressure," she says. "I hope everyone has someone they can talk to about everything, without being judged. I've always had my sister and some friends. You can talk to parents, teachers, coaches, a sports psychologist, but friends who don't judge you are in a separate category. My sister has been that kind of a friend, too."

Regrets and doubts are also high on her list.

"Try not to regret anything, or do things you will regret. If you have the slightest doubt about doing something you think you might regret, don't do it. For instance, all athletes think about quitting, from time to time. Don't make up your mind about things like that too fast."

Bad Days

"If I have a bad day - a really bad day - I ask myself why, so I won't have another day like that. Also, I use music to get me out of that bad day. I scream it out. I sing and move with music all the time. Listening to my iPod on the subway, I can't keep still, like most of the rest of the people on the subway in Toronto. My singing is horrible, my sister says. She's a real singer. I listen to Green Day, a lot, and Our Lady Peace."

Music

"Instead of looking for new music by my favourite bands, I just listen to songs I like and find out whose song it is later. I like everything, even rap, especially Alternative, but not heavy rock. The lyrics get my attention but it's the beat that grabs me first."

Journal

"I also journal it out. My journal is crazy, all over the place, full of things I write down instead of saying them to anyone. It's full of my hopes, dreams, insecurities, self-conscious moments about my weight or whatever. I have my moments. Writing about these things calms me down."

"I read over past entries, trying to learn all about what caused me to have a bad day, because I don't want to go there again. Reading them over, I've realized there are times when training was a waste of time. I could have sat at home, instead of training, since I was having one bad day after another."

"My journal is a good place for me to get out the anger

I feel at coaches, or whoever. We don't talk back to our coaches. I write it out, instead."

Don't Stop

"Athletes get so annoyed with themselves for things like that. In rhythmic gymnastics, the music never stops, during a competition, so that's the way we train, at my club. The music doesn't stop if you drop something, even though you might want to start over. You can't stop and rewind during a competition. Some coaches stop the music, during training, but I wouldn't recommend that."

Injuries And Luck

"Alex has been very lucky as she has had very few injuries," her mother says. "In the past two years, she had a few more than before."

Princesses

"Something is always hurting," her mother reports. "Alex just says, 'Oh well, I have to suck it up and not be a princess'."

Training

"I train at a gym, as well as my club, and I work out alongside some of the members of the Canadian women's hockey team. We work out at the Fitness Institute. It's arranged by the Canadian Olympic Committee. It's fun to have people the same age to work out with, other athletes, in different sports, because we can relate."

Cool And Down To Earth

"I met a skater at the gym who won a bronze medal at

the Olympics," Alex says. "I'm in awe of the hockey players on Canada's women's team, who also work out there. They are so cool and down to earth. Other people, who aren't competitive athletes, train alongside of them without recognizing them."

Making Contact

"I've learned to love public speaking," Alexandra Orlando says. "Lots of impromptu interviews have taught me how to do that. Since the Commonwealth Games, the media has gone crazy and my phone is always ringing. I've learned to be comfortable in front of the camera. I'm interested in being a motivational speaker, too," she adds. "I'd love to go to high schools to talk to kids and motivate them. I think they need young people to speak to them and I hope I have that opportunity. When you're 15 or 16, you aren't interested in what anyone more than a few years older than you says."

Zen And The Art Of Rhythmic Gymnastics

"I visualize a perfect performance the night before a big event and just live it in the moment when it's time to compete. The night before a competition, I visualize my performance, with everything going perfectly. That's it."

Sports Psychology

"I've talked to a sports psychologist. That's very important and useful for an athlete. It's good to have someone to discuss things with in addition to coaches and parents. We discussed visualization but I don't really do it. I know I'll put all my energy into it and be very focused on that 1.5 minutes on the carpet."

Focus

"I don't use visualization during a competition. I live it

in the moment."

Breathing And Balance

"My routine for the final moments before a competition is well known to my coach. She gives me a moment, all to myself, just before it's my turn to perform. I close my eyes, get my balance, breathe, but I don't visualize. Breathing is very important."

The Ritual

"At the last second, my coach always says the same thing to me, which is a kind of short-hand or point-form for things we've discussed. She says, "Calm. Focus. Watch. Be strong"."

"When she says, "Watch", that means, "Watch your apparatus". Keeping track of your apparatus is very important in my sport. If you're working with a hoop, you have to make sure you've got it, when you think you've got it, and not go on without it. One mistake leads to another and that leads to another, in rhythmic gymnastics. If you make one mistake, you know what it can lead to, so you tend to get rattled. I used to get rattled. That used to be my main problem. Now, I know one mistake is okay. But a series of mistakes in quick succession can drop you from 10th place to 30th in a second."

Martin Avery's Afterword

At the time of this writing, "Alex the Great" has cracked the top 15 in rhythmic gymnastics in the world and is moving in on the top ten. She is already regarded as the best in the world in ribbon, which is a key event in the competitions in her sport.

I asked her coach, the president of her club, her mom and dad, about Alex's chances of winning a medal at the Beijing Olympics in 2008. They all used the term "incredible long shot".

That phrase always makes me think of the movies "Million Dollar Baby" and "Sea Biscuit".

Even more than those sports movies about overcoming incredible odds, Alexandra's journey makes me think of the Cinderella story. There are no cinders or evil sisters in the story of Alex the Great, but the archetypal pattern is similar. Cinderella works hard, gets to go to the ball, thanks to her fairy godmother, has to leave the ball early, without the prince, and loses her slipper. Later, she has another chance, the slipper fits, and her wildest dreams come true.

Alex has worked incredibly hard for over a decade, training and competing, in inadequate facilities at home and in palaces of sport around the world. With the help of her mother, as well as her coach and her club, not to mention her father, who has been a prince, she earned a spot at the last Olympics, but then had it snatched away, at the last second. She didn't quit. She trained harder, at higher levels of difficulty, became Canada's national champion five years in a row, earned a record six gold medals at the Commonwealth Games in Australia. She proved the shoe fits. Now she's on her way to the Olympics, again.

The Alex I've come to know is much more of a fighter than Cinderella. She doesn't just wish upon a star. Imagine Cinderella as a tomboy, growing into a woman who has the attributes of a great athlete but still loves to dress up and dance like a fairy.

The idea that 'Cinderella' embodies myth elements was explored in <u>The Uses of Enchantment</u> by Bruno Bettelheim. The term Cinderella has evolved from its story-book beginnings to become the name for a variety of female personalities. Some girls are described as a Cinderella if they are meek and submissive to orders. That's not Alexandra Orlando. Others are called Cinderella if they tend to quietly complain. For example, a girl from a wealthy household who has been ordered to wash the dishes as a fulfillment of her once-a-month chores would be deemed a Cinderella; a fallen princess who has finally met with tough reality. That's not Alexandra, either.

Many see Cinderella's personality or actions in a negative light. She has come under criticism as more confrontational and headstrong heroines have become the new ideal of what a women is expected to be in American culture. Cinderella has many admirable qualities, taking a more calm and discreet approach in fulfilling her wishes. That sounds more like Alex.

Even more than Cinderella, Alex reminds me of my number one Canadian hero, Dr. Norman Bethune. She has his determination, his ability to overcome great obstacles and beat the odds, and she's going to China.

If you ask me, "Will Alexandra Orlando win a medal at the next Olympics?", I'd say the spark and fire of Alex the Great and how it is ignited by competition in her chosen sport - the sport that seems to have chosen her - and I can see Alexandra Orlando, the rhythmic gymnast from Canada, of all places, larger than her Eastern European competition, larger than life, climbing that Olympic podium in Beijing, China, with the Canadian flag behind her, and the ecstatic expression of a great winner lighting up her beautiful face with that megawatt smile of hers.

Let me be the first to predict an Olympic medal for Alex the Great rhythmic gymnast from Canada.

Appendix: The Ultimate Guide To Rhythmic Gymnastics For Dummies And Idiots

A perfect fusion of athletics and aesthetics, gymnastics ranks among the defining sports of the Olympic Games. Rhythmic Gymnastics is quite possibly the most beautiful of all competitive sports. Soccer is called 'the beautiful game', but how can soccer players compete with rhythmic gymnastics? It choreographs creative movements to music, while working with ribbon, balls, hoops, ropes and clubs in a dance-and-tumble routine that is all about developing personal style and the ability to get one's own artistic message and charisma across to the audience.

Also, there's no head-butting.

Don't let the colourful ribbon, ball and hoop fool you. Rhythmic gymnastics is a demanding sport in which athletes twist themselves into poses the ordinary human would find impossible, all while keeping control of the ribbon, ball, hoop and clubs, to music, with a very limited amount of time. Try to forget the fact they do all that while wearing beautiful costumes, not to mention the make-up.

The Art of Constructing A Championship Composition For Rhythmic Gymnastics

You have 1.5 minutes - just 90 seconds - to move with the music, across the entire carpet, alternating all the elements of rhythmic gymnastics - apparatus, costumes, presence, et cetera - for points in a competition.

How do you order all those elements over that limited time in that space?

The goal of choreography, for rhythmic gymnastics, is to keep the spectators in mind. Your routine is a performance art piece. It has to have unity, a single style, for integrity, from the beginning to the end, or from the introductory pose to the final pose. A strong start and a brilliant finish, connected gracefully by all your elements, in a brief but intense composition, is the ideal.

Your routine depends heavily on the music you have chosen so carefully, after listening to a lot of music, over and over, and rehearsing to that music hundreds of times.

A rhythmic gymnastics routine has to have variety, with changing speed, direction, amplitude, strength, at different levels, from lying on the floor to leaping in the air, organized in a way that strengthens the artistic impression.

Including more difficult elements that are unique and original, particularly at the end of the routine, after leading up to them with an increasing tempo, makes a great impression on spectators. But how about the judges?

Rhythmic Gymnastics is quite possibly the most beautiful of all competitive sports. Competitors must use the apparatus of rhythmic gymnastics - the rope, hoop, ball, clubs and ribbon - so skillfully they appear to be an extension of their bodies and they must incorporate them into routines always accompanied by music.

This question has too often been asked of rhythmic gymnastics: Is it Dance? Is it Art? Or is it Sport? In reality it is a unique combination of the best of all three worlds. It is athletic performance art, or performance art for athletes.

The essence of rhythmic gymnastics, some would argue, is self-expression. Without the extremely difficult acrobatic elements used in artistic gymnastics, the movements in rhythmic gymnastics are elegant, expressive, precise and graceful. Athletes require a full range of flexibility throughout the body, in addition to explosive power. It is both of those factors combined that allows athletes to maintain perfect body alignment in leaps, balances, pirouettes and other intricate body movements.

Rhythmic gymnastic athletes display artistic coordination and cohesion in their use of the hand apparatus with rhythmic sensibility while taking risks with technical precision. The highest-level competitors take great pride in their original compositions as they appear to become one with the music and the apparatus.

Women's artistic gymnastics is quite different than rhythmic gymnastics. Artistic gymnastics includes uneven bars, balance beam, vault and floor exercise. Many of the moves in rhythmic gymnastics are borrowed from classical ballet. The main difference between artistic gymnastics and rhythmic gymnastics, according to some of the experts, is that acrobatic skills are not allowed in rhythmic gymnastics.

"Artistic gymnastics is not as good for the body as rhythmic gymnastics," Mimi Masleva says. "Injuries in artistic gymnastics can be life-threatening or life-changing. They are like circus artists working without the protection given in the circus. It is better for the guys who do artistic gymnastics but not so great for the women. It seems to stunt their growth. The constant pounding and all the tumbling seems to have given them all the same profile, with the exception of one tall Russian."

Only women compete in rhythmic gymnastics. The competitors can compete individually or as a team. Gymnasts perform on a carpet to music doing leaps, pivots, balances, and other elements to demonstrate flexibility and coordination.

There are two different types of competition in Rhythmic Gymnastics: Individual and Group. In the Group Competition, five athletes work together as one. They use one of the hand apparatus or a combination of two different pieces, such as ribbon and hoops. To watch the combination of five different personalities meld together to perform intricate compositions involving high flying throws and exchanges is truly thrilling. The element of cooperation among the athletes is essential resulting in a breathtaking, harmonious unit.

Rhythmic gymnastics is a sport for girls and women, primarily. It is growing in popularity in North America and Japan, is already very popular in Latin America and Malaysia, and is enormously popular in Europe, especially the Eastern European countries, particularly Estonia and Bulgaria, as well as Russia.

Alex's father, Paul Orlando, is convinced the sport called rhythmic gymnastics has had an enormously positive impact on his daughter. "Alex is amazing and it has a lot to do with rhythmic gymnastics," he says. "This sport did a lot for her. She can now speak in front of thousands without being flustered. She can walk into a room, talk to anyone, without any fear. She is smart but this sport gave her confidence. And it wasn't all the winning, so much; that's the end result."

Rhythmic gymnastics is an artistic sport designed for females, oriented toward grace, smoothness, and connection to music, and it is judged by a code of points. It involves body movement and apparatus handling. Single competitors or groups of two or more manipulate five types of apparatus, combining elements of ballet, gymnastics, and theatrical dance, with apparatus manipulation. The victor is the participant who earns the most points, as awarded by a panel of judges, for leaps, balances, pivots, flexibility, apparatus handling and artistic effect.

Rhythmic gymnastics combines ballet and creative movements to music, while working with ribbon, balls, hoops, ropes and clubs in a choreographed dance-and-tumble routine. It has a lot more dance than artistic gymnastics. Everything is done on the floor with far different routines and different music. Rhythmic gymnastics includes ball, hoop, ribbon, rope, clubs and sometimes floor exercise.

This gymnastics sport combines elements of floor exercise, dance, and apparatus handling, choreographed with music. The sport requires a very high skill level for balance, turns, pivots, and many other acrobatic movements. It is an artistic sport, presented in beautifully decorated costumes or 'competition suits', and requires the ability to use the apparatus, with a smooth musical flow, and presentation.

As in ballet, technique is extremely important in rhythmic gymnastics. Rhythmic gymnastic routines are performed on a carpet 13 metres square, or just over 40 feet, in a room with a very high ceiling, and each routine takes 90 seconds, or a minute and a half. Each apparatus has to be coordinated with the movements and the music in ways that show versatility, ambidexterity, and volume, as well as amplitude. Rhythmic gymnasts also demonstrate speed, strength, and endurance, while performing.

They perform compositions which showcase their grace and skill and somehow the good rhythmic gymnasts make all that look easy.

For competitive rhythmic gymnastics, the rules and requirements for all the elements involved in the sport are very specific. They have been set by the Fédération

Internationale de Gymnastique, also known as the FIG, which is the governing body for the sport internationally.

In the individual event they perform different routines with four of the five apparatus. In the team competition, teams of five perform together once using clubs and once with two using hoops and three using ribbon.

How does one become a rhythmic gymnast? Anyone can become a rhythmic gymnast. Some people get started through artistic gymnastics - with the bars and beam - or through ballet. Mary Sanders, Erika-Leigh Stirton, and many other famous rhythmic gymnasts started with artistic gymnastics. Mary and Erika were both told they did not have the right body type for artistic gymnastics. Coaches tend to look for a girl who is tall and lean. In rhythmic gymnastics, the athletes are bent into positions the typical human would find impossible. Is that why they're looking for people who are tall or lean. It has to do with presentation. There are rhythmic gymnasts who do well who aren't tall and skinny, but they are the exceptions. In addition, you have to be very flexible. You have to be somewhat flexible, naturally, and then work on that. You overstretch and overstretch a little more every day, and eventually that kind of flexibility comes.

Rhythmic gymnastics is renowned for its charm, its fluidity. Rhythmic gymnastics is an exclusive female discipline, with individual and collective events. It embodies many classic ballet movements. But where did it come from?

A Brief History Of Rhythmic Gymnastics

The word 'gymnastics' came from the word 'gymnazein', which meant 'exercising without clothes'.

Gymnastics has existed for more than 2000 years, but has only been a competitive sport for a little over 100 years.

Rhythmic gymnastics started as a competitive sport in the early 1950s. Then in 1963 the first world championships were held in Europe. In 1984 the sport entered the Olympic Games for the first time.

In 1984, rhythmic gymnastics achieved full Olympic status at the Games in Los Angeles. The first ever Olympic gold medal in rhythmic gymnastics was won by Canada's Lori Fung. The first World Championships for individual gymnasts took place in 1963 in Budapest, Hungary. Groups were introduced at the same level in 1967 in Copenhagen, Denmark. When rhythmic gymnastics was added to the 1984 Summer Olympics in Los Angeles, with an Individual All-around competition, many federations from the Eastern European countries were forced to boycott.

The first Canadian to ever win a medal at a Rhythmic Gymnastics World Cup was Ontario's Mary Fuzesi in 1990.

Rhythmic gymnastics was recognized by the International Gymnastics Federation in 1963. In 1996, the rhythmic group event was added as a medal sport at the Olympic Games.

Unlike Artistic Gymnastics, Rhythmic Gymnastics is currently performed in official competition by women only. It began to be practiced in the 19th century with basic choreographies and it was known as group gymnastics. As the complexity of the choreographies were enhanced, from the end of the World War I, the interest and the enchantment of the audience also grew, until the discipline was recognized by the International Gymnastics Federation in 1962.

When rhythmic gymnastics first caught the attention of the Fédération Internationale de Gymnastique (FIG) in the middle of the 20th century, its devotees were calling it 'modern gymnastics'. Its hazy history can clearly be traced back to previous centuries. Gymnastics, rhythmic and artistic combined, started in Europe during the eighteenth century as one sport and over time gradually developed into two different yet similar sports.

Rhythmic gymnastics grew out of the 19th-century Swedish system of free exercise developed by Peter Henry Ling, who promoted 'aesthetic gymnastics,' in which students expressed their feelings and emotions through bodily movement. This idea was extended by Catherine E. Beecher, who founded the Western Female Institute in Ohio, USA, in 1837.

In Beecher's gymnastics program, called *grace without dancing*, the young women exercised to music, moving from simple calisthenics to more strenuous activities. During the 1880s, Emil Dalcroze of Switzerland developed eurhythmics, a form of physical training for musicians and dancers. George Demeny of France created exercises to music that were designed to promote grace of movement, muscular flexibility, and good posture.

All of these styles were combined around 1900 into the Swedish school of rhythmic gymnastics, which would later add dance elements from Finland. Around this time, Ernest Idla of Estonia established a degree of difficulty for each movement.

Rhythmic gymnastics as a sport began in the 1940s in the former Soviet Union. It was there that for the first time, the spirit of sports was combined with the sensuous art of classical ballet. Isadora Duncan gets credit for the famous rebellion against the dogma of classical ballet and the shift toward the creation of a new discipline that would blend art and sport.

Rhythmic gymnastics started as an independent competitive sport in the early 1950s by the Russians. In 1963, the first rhythmic gymnastics world championship was held in

Europe. Although rhythmic gymnastics has its own world championships, it did not become an Olympic medal sport until 1984. This is partly why rhythmic gymnastics is such a little known and hardly recognized sport in North America.

The FIG recognized this discipline in 1961, first as modern gymnastics, then as rhythmic sportive gymnastics, and finally as rhythmic gymnastics. The first World Championships for individual gymnasts took place in 1963 in Budapest, Hungary. FIG was formed on 23 July 1881 when representatives of the gymnastics associations of Belgium, France and the Netherlands met in Liège. As a governing body, FIG is held in high esteem by both its member federations and gymnastics clubs throughout the world or, as they like to say, all five continents.

In 1897, 17 national associations joined together to form the basis of the European Gymnastics Federation. However, when the USA was admitted in 1921, the Committee changed its name to the Fédération Internationale de Gymnastique or FIG, as it is known today.

FIG comprises three Olympic disciplines: artistic, rhythmic and trampoline. Each discipline is controlled by a Technical Committee made up of a Technical President and six members. The Technical Committees are responsible for the coordination and control of their specific discipline in terms of the technical requirements for competition as they relate to each specific discipline.

At the end of 2006, the International Federation of Gymnastics relocated its headquarters from Moutier to Neuchâtel. The decision to make the move was made at the FIG's 2005 meeting in Baku, Azerbaijan.

The FIG receives revenues from the Olympic Games and from television licenses. That is the where their operational budget comes from and also other funds which are redistributed by the FIG to its various programs in Development and Education.

During the Olympiad years, the FIG spends several million Swiss francs on these programs, training coaches, athletes, and judges, and providing assistance for equipping gymnastics halls.

Albania, Mongolia, Argentina, Morocco, Latvia are among the many nations that have recently received gymnastic apparatus from the FIG. Senegal and the City of Thies received funds from their own governments to build a new gymnastics hall, which was then equipped through the support given by the FIG. That made it possible for Thies to host the African Championships of Gymnastics in the fall of 2005.

The revenues of the FIG are also allocated to the FIG Academy, an educational program for training educators. Significant sums of Swiss francs are spent around the world, on each continent, on the education of coaches in the seven disciplines of the FIG. The organization looks after gymnastics, artistic gymnastics for men and women, trampoline, aerobic, and acrobatic gymnastics, and rhythmic gymnastics.

Rhythmic gymnastics had its Olympic debut in 1984 in Los Angeles. Rhythmic gymnastics was added to the Summer Olympics with an Individual All-around competition. However, many federations from the Eastern European countries were forced to boycott.

A Canadian was the first rhythmic gymnast to earn an Olympic gold medal. Lori Fung was awarded the gold medal with a score of 57.9 out of a possible 80 in the competition, which included the hoop, ball, clubs, and ribbon.

At those Olympics the final scores were the total of the scores from two rounds.

In the 1996 Olympic Games, in Atlanta, the scoring system was changed. The scores of the first round were not added to the scores of the final round and the apparatus included were the rope, ball, clubs, and ribbon.

At the 1996 Games, group competition was also added.

History Of Hoops, Balls, Ribbon, And Clubs

Each apparatus used in rhythmic gymnastics has a history of its own.

The rope was recognized by the Federation of International Gymnastics in 1965.

The ribbon is widely used in traditional Chinese dance, became popular with rhythmic gymnasts in the 1940s, and was included in the World Championships for rhythmic gymnastics in 1971.

The clubs, once a weapon and then a symbol of authority in Eastern European countries, have been used as gymnastics apparatus since sometime in the middle of the 1900s, and have been part of the World Championships since 1973.

The ball has been used in physical education as long as the rope and was included in the very first World Championships, back in 1963.

The hoop has been popular since the 1930s and was recognized by the FIG in 1963.

The Magic Carpet

The apparatus used in rhythmic gymnastics - the hoop, ball, rope, clubs, and ribbon - are featured in separate routines. In addition, a free floor exercise is also performed at certain levels of competition. All the exercises are performed on a carpeted floor that measures 13 metres square (42' 8") with a 50 cm (1' 8") border. The overall size is 14 m square (45' 11"). There should also be a two-metre safety zone around the carpet. The total size required, including the safety zone, is a minimum of 18 metres or close to 60 feet. The floor, or carpet size, has changed, over the years. The carpet used for rhythmic gymnastics is now the same size as the carpet used for artistic gymnastics, but it has a smaller safety border. The carpet may or may not be lightly padded. The outer edge of the carpet's border marking is defined as 'out of bounds'.

The ceiling is important in this sport. Because of the high tosses used with the apparatus, a ceiling height of ten to 12 metres is recommended. A ceiling height of a minimum of eight metres, or 26' 3", is required for international competitions.

Soft And Rigid Apparatus

The apparatus can be split into two groups: the soft and the rigid. The rope and the ribbon are considered soft and the hoop, ball, and clubs are referred to as rigid.

Clubs are always used in pairs and are called twin apparatus.

The hoop size must be from 80-90 cm, or 31.2" to 35.1", measured at the inner diameter. It must weigh at least 300 grams. For the children's division, it is 60 to 90 cm. diameter and 150 grams. There is no maximum weight specified. The hoop is often decorated with brightly colored tapes to provide a pleasing appearance and the tapes are included when calculating the weight.

The ball must have a diameter of 18 to 20 cm, and must also weigh more than 400 grams, for seniors, and 200 grams for children. The diameter of the ball is 14 to 20 cm. for children. The colour may be anything, including a mixture of colours, but not gold, silver or bronze. The ball may be made of rubber or plastic.

The clubs are made out of wood or plastic and must be between 40 and 50 cm in length, weighing in at least 150 grams each. For the children's division, the length is between 25 and 50 cm, and each club weighs a minimum of 75 grams. The club has a shape similar to that of a bottle. Hard rubber clubs are in common usage but are not specified in the FIG norms.

The rope is made from hemp or a synthetic material. The length is optional and varies, depending on what feels right for the gymnast. The length of the rope is proportional to the height of the gymnast. While standing on the middle of the rope, its ends should reach the armpits. The rope may be thicker in the middle. Its thickness must be uniform but it can be reinforced in the center. Knots and handles are also optional. It may be wrapped with a thin, non-slip, material corresponding to the width of the hand. Colour is optional, so long as it is visible.

The ribbon is usually made of silk or polyester, and must be six metres long for the elite gymnast. For the Junior level gymnast the ribbon may be a minimum of five metres (that's more than 15 feet), and four metres for the Novice or Children's level. The ribbon is attached to the stick by means of a thread, nylon cord or rings. The stick, including the attachment to the ribbon, is 50 to 60 cm. and can have ten cm of anti-slip tape or rubber at the level of the grip.

The material of the ribbon is satin or synthetic satin; any color except gold, silver or bronze is allowed. The ribbon weight is a minimum of 35 grams. A cane is attached to one end of the ribbon to help with tosses and patterns. The cane must be 50 to 60 cm in length and a maximum diameter of ten cm. It is attached to a stick of wood, or synthetic material, one centimetre wide, and 50 to 60 centimetres long, in a cylindrical or conical shape. A ring attaches the ribbon to the stick. The connection hardware between the cane and ribbon (a swivel mechanism) must not exceed seven centimetres in length.

Rhythmic gymnasts polish all their movements, especially the many small movements required for mastering the apparatus. Judges look at grips of all kinds, which they say can make or break a performance. How the athlete holds the hoop, ball, clubs, rope, and ribbon is as important as how they throw them, catch them, and bounce them - if they bounce.

The main apparatus grips are the one-handed and two-handed, the straight, reverse, and crossed, and they may be from below, above, the sides or, for hoop, folded rope and the ribbon, from the inside. There are also atypical apparatus grips, using the forearms, shoulders, feet, legs, thigh, back, stomach, and the areas between the various parts of the body.

For clubs, there is a rigid grip and a free grip. The clubs can be held by the same or different grips, be released with different swings, pass under the arms, legs, or shoulders, be symmetrical or asymmetrical when thrown, moved in the same or other directions, at the same or other heights and ranges, and they can be rotated during flights.

Rhythmic gymnasts study the physics of bounces and rebounds for clubs and ropes as well as for hoops and balls. They also study the physics of rolls, for hoops and balls, and the physics of wrapping, for ribbon, and the physics of rotations, for hoops.

Ribbon makes snakes, spirals, and figure eights that are vertical or horizontal, in front of their bodies, over their heads, and at their sides, in patterns that must appear natural but not languid. They may be big, small, or medium in size and they cannot ever touch the carpet.

Ropes are moved in figure eights, snakes, spirals, mills, and sails.

Group Competition

In the Group Competition, five athletes work together as one. They use one of the hand apparatus or a combination of two different pieces, such as ribbon and hoops.

To watch the combination of five different personalities meld together for rhythmic gymnastics group competitions, performing intricate compositions involving high throws of the apparatus, and exchanges, is both beautiful and thrilling. The cooperation of the athletes results in a breathtaking, harmonious unit. It looks as though they share one mind or have extra sensory perception, in addition to their many athletic gifts. It is awe-inspiring.

Judging History For Rhythmic Gymnastics

The sport's governing body, the FIG, changed the Code of Points in 2001, 2003 and 2005 to emphasize technical elements and reduce the subjectivity of judging.

Before 2001, judging was on a scale of ten like that of artistic gymnastics. It was changed to a 30-point scale in 2003 and in 2005 was changed to 20. There are three values adding up to be the final points - technical, artistic and execution.

International competitions are split between Juniors, girls under 15; and Seniors, for girls 15 and over. Gymnasts typically start training at a very young age and those at their peak are typically in their late teens or early twenties.

The largest events in the sport are the Olympic Games, World Championships, and Grand-Prix Tournaments.

Rhythmic gymnastics is largely a sport for women and

girls, but a growing number of men participate. The Japanese version of Men's rhythmic gymnastics includes tumbling and is performed on a spring floor. Points are awarded based on a ten-point scale that measures the level of difficulty of the tumbling and apparatus handling. Japan hosted the first men's world championships in 2003, drawing teams from Canada, Korea, Malaysia, and the United States.

Marisa Orlando says, "The Bulgarian coaches brought out the beauty and the passion of this sport. The rules of the game have changed, over the years, and for a while there was the biggest emphasis on the technical side, but that has changed. It has been difficult for the girls to bring out the beauty in the sport, but some have managed to do it."

"Now, the sport is more artistic," she says, "and that's a good thing. It makes the sport more interesting for the girls. This year, competitions were very nice to watch as they were a little less technically oriented, a little more athletic, and the girls were able to bring out the beauty of the sport again."

"Costumes were plain and simple, years ago, when this sport was getting started," she adds. "Then, little stones were allowed, as decoration. Now it's like Las Vegas out there. That started about four years ago. At the 2003 Worlds, in Budapest, I noticed it starting to change. Now anything goes."

The costumes used in rhythmic gymnastics now look more like the women's costumes in figure skating and ice dance.

"New suits cost, on average, $1,200.00 each. The average good suit will run from $600.00 and up. We paid $1,200.00 because of all the extra crystals on it. A lot of the expense is the stones, as they have to be glued on, one by one," Marisa Orlando explains. "There are four suits needed for each competition, so the total cost is around five thousand dollars. The costumes, or competition suits, we're having made now will last through 2007, for the world qualifier events. If she goes to the Olympics, we'll have to have new suits made for Beijing."

How To Score Points With Rhythmic Gymnastics Judges

"Too many judges are fooled into thinking a smile equals style."
~Neshka Robeva
Bulgarian rhythmic gymnastics coach

"At the Olympics, there was a little bit of unfair judging, but I tried not to be disappointed and to do my best. I think the audience respected and loved what I did at the Olympics, and that helped me become the world champion in 1997."
~Elena Vitrichenko
in International Gymnast Magazine 1999

"Now, the judges are God; I'm not. I can fly like a bird or dance like a flower, but the judges say who is the winner and who is not."
~Amina Zaripova
from International Gymnast Magazine, March 1999

"The Russian girls in rhythmic gymnastics are very good technically," Marisa Orlando says. "In Maria Petrova's time, they were fantastic, technically. The Bulgarians have brought passion and artistry into the sport."

The sport is extremely challenging for many reasons, including the fact that the music and the apparatus have to go together so well, she explains. "It has to look as though the apparatus is attached to you by a magnet. It has to look like the ball is part of you."

New Rules

"The new rules of her sport make it better for Alex. Instead of competition number one being used for judging, they will use competition number two, and that is her better competition." says Marisa Orlando.

Points

The Code Of Points classifies the rhythmic gymnastics' athlete's body movements in fundamental and other groups with different levels of difficulty. The fundamental group includes jumps and leaps, balances, pivots, and flexibility and waves. The four groups include traveling, skips and hops, swings and circles, and turns. There are four levels of difficulty: A, B, C, and D. The most difficult level is 'D'.

This list of what the judges are looking for, when awarding points, also serves as a good description of what rhythmic gymnasts are trying to do on the carpet.

The Body Movements

As well as the jumps and leaps, balances, turns and pivots, body waves and swings, there are a number of floor elements, including rolls, walkovers, cartwheels, passing supports, grovels, turns, lying positions, and others.

Balances are moves with one leg or both legs on the floor. Turns and pivots describe movements with one or both legs with body rotations. Body waves and swings are movements without rotations.

There are static positions and dynamic, or moving, positions. The dynamic positions may be done with or without rotations.

There are linking elements, also called modal elements, including poses and traveling.

Traveling means running and walking, as opposed to poses, used at the start and the finish of a program.

The expressive elements are arm waves and swings.

All of the elements performed by the rhythmic gymnasts are supposed to demonstrate the correct shape of the legs, feet, hands, and toes, as well as correct body posture and good amplitude.

And amplitude is the ability to use the highest degree of flexibility.

The hips, the spine, and all joints are supposed to display exceptional amplitude.

Flight is the term used to describe jumps and leaps. Jumps involve take-offs from both feet and usually have a steep trajectory. Leaps usually involve take-offs from one leg; their trajectories are more curved.

Flight is examined closely and the take-off, main phase, and landing are all important.

There are many types of jumps and leaps, including the vertical, cat, scissors, tuck, Cossack, hop, arch, cabriole, pike, straddle or stride, stag, ring, split, open, jete, and butterfly, as well as a jump in arabesque. There are variations of each of those jumps and leaps, with take-offs from one or both legs, turns or half-turns.

There is a front split, a side split, a split leap with a half turn, a split leap with a change of legs, the knocking split leap, and a knocking leap with a ring.

A cabriole is a jump with the legs coming together in flight. The Cossack jump has one leg straight and the other moving into the tuck position.

Balances are also important and must be held on one or both legs, without stepping or hopping, or using an apparatus or hands, in a well-defined shape for one second.

Balances may be performed on the knees, as well.

The terms arabesque and attitude both come from classical ballet. An attitude is performed with the athlete's free leg bent or held in front of the body. An arabesque has the free leg fully stretched and lifted behind the body.

There are four arabesques and two attitudes.

There are front balances, side balances, back balances, combination balances, balances with a change in the trunk's position, balances with a change of position of the free leg, and balances with a change in the position of both the trunk and the free leg.

A pivot is also called a pirouette and has more rotations than a turn. Turns and pivots must be performed on the toes, with good amplitude, with well-defined shapes, and the athlete has to keep her balance.

There are small pivots, grand pivots, and regular pivots, as well as combination pivots.

There are stepping turns, chain turns, cross turns, and spiral turns.

When it comes to swings and body waves, there are moves made by the entire body or only by the trunk, and they may be done to the side, forward, in reverse.

Floor Elements

The basic floor elements are rolls, walkovers, cartwheels, passing supports, grovels, lying positions, floor balancing, floor turns, slides, wave-like motions, and floor jumps.

There are many types of rolls from the forward roll through the neck and the backward roll through the neck to the forward roll through one shoulder, and the lateral roll in the tuck position or split position.

A walkover is a handspring movement and there are

several types including forward, backward, and Arabian.

Passing supports are movements with both legs lift, without flight, using the hands, or one hand, or forearms, or chest, for support. There is the passing support on one hand with a split, backward passing support on one hand, passing support on the shoulder.

Grovels are like lateral rolls but the arms are used to support the body.

Static poses are judged on aesthetics, the character of the musical accompaniment, subsequent movements, previous movements, individuality, imagination, and the plan of the composition. Static poses include standing, kneeling, sitting, squatting, semi-squatting, lunging, balancing on supports, and lying.

Traveling has many steps, including steps on toes, soft steps, high steps, sharp steps, wide steps, spring steps, cross steps, and running.

There are also isolations, taken from jazz, meaning one part of the body moves in one direction while other body parts move in the opposite direction.

Wave-like motions include arm waves, hand waves, swaying and swinging. Spring like motions require bending and extending.

The various kinds of apparatus have different movements associated with them. When using the rope, there are swings, in various directions, over, around, under the gymnast's body. The gymnast can also throw and catch the rope, toss it, perform balances with it, and perform many other movements.

Snakes, spirals, swings, throws and catches, traps, figure eights, and circles are all executed with ribbon. You can also wrap it around yourself.

Swinging, throws and catches, circling, clapping, trapping, spinning are the movements associated with the clubs. Rolling, swinging, throwing and catching, bouncing, balancing, and trapping are movements associated with the ball. Rolling, swinging, throwing and catching, jumping (over, under, through), circling, trapping, and spinning are the movements associated with hoops.

The movements associated with floor exercise are, well, almost anything!

For group routines, the leotards worn by the gymnasts must be identical material, color and style for all members. Leotards may be any color except gold, silver or bronze. Solid or patterns are allowed; the pattern is restricted to stripes, geometrical design or flowers. No decoration or trim on the leotard is allowed. The cut of the leotard at the top of the leg cannot go beyond the fold of the crotch.

Leotards may be with or without sleeves; the dance-leotards with the narrow straps are not allowed. Transparent materials are not used; long tights down to the ankles of one color, over or under the leotard are permitted. Only a unitard of one color from the waist to the ankles is allowed. The neckline in back cannot go beyond the center point between the shoulder blades, and in front it must not go too low. Points are deducted for violations.

Hairstyles are also regulated. Briefly stated, the hair must be neat. Footwear is bare feet or gymnastic-style slippers.

The group exercise consists of four to five gymnasts doing a routine at the same time with each other. They may all use the same apparatus or they could have different apparatus at the same time. One of the goals of group rhythmic gymnastics is to have all the gymnasts doing the movements at the same time. They also have to exchange apparatus with each other and meet other requirements. Of course they must have the same good quality of movement to music, grace, flexibly and difficulty as you have to have in individual rhythmic gymnastics routines.

Individual rhythmic gymnastic music for routines has a time maximum of 90 seconds. Group music has a maximum of 150 seconds. In rhythmic gymnastics there are many rules such as: after you begin performing your routine, you or your apparatus cannot go out of the marked area without points being deducted; your outfit and apparatus can not be gold, silver, or bronze colored or you will be deducted for it; if you drop your apparatus you will be deducted. There are a lot more rules, some of them are not very rational. For instance, you will be deducted if you wear jewelry, if you change your outfit between routines (and are below level eight), if your hair thing doesn't match your outfit or apparatus, if your outfit comes below your shoulders in the back or above your hipbone in the front. Some of the rules may seem irrelevant, even ridiculous, but they all have their reasons.

The level a gymnast is at is determined by her skills and her coach. Beginning in 2001, upward mobility was influenced by a qualifying All-around score during a sanctioned event. An AA score of 30 is recommended to move to the next level. At the coaches discretion the appropriate level for the gymnast can be selected.

Competitions are normally held between levels, and similar age brackets. That is each level may have competitions of juniors against juniors, seniors against seniors, etc. In an invitational meet, age brackets may be ignored.

A gymnast's age bracket changes on January 1 in the year she becomes eligible for that bracket, not on her birthday. For example, if the birth date is December 25, 1992, that gymnast will compete as a senior (15 and up) in year 2007. Novice are ages nine to 11; Juniors are 12 to 14; and Seniors are 15 and up.

In 2005 the minimum age for seniors increased to 16 in the year they compete.

Rules

Rhythmic Gymnastics involves performing to music with one of five apparatus - rope, hoop, clubs, ball and ribbon. There is an individual event and a team event. Gymnasts gain points from the judges for their leaps, balance, flexibility, pivots, handling of the apparatus and artistic effect.

The gymnasts are expected to use the entire floor area in their routines and their work with each apparatus should be equally balanced in each hand. The apparatus should also be kept moving at all times or points will be deducted.

Judging rhythmic gymnastics is subjective, as is figure skating, and in both sports the judges' decisions are influenced by the individual athlete's history, at competitions.

"We will have to see how the judges treat Alex this year," Marisa Orlando says. "Sometimes you have to pay your dues along the way. The European judges love Alex more and more, especially since her success at the Commonwealth Games in Australia."

"The politics of judging in our sport seem to be something like the politics involved in judging figure skating," Alexandra Orlando says. "It is more complicated due to the fact Canada has no judge, sometimes, at international competitions. Sometimes, if there is a Canadian judge, that person has relatively little influence with the other judges. That makes it more challenging for a Canadian athlete to compete, perhaps, but that changes over time."

Although she has sometimes been surprised or disappointed by the scores given by judges, Alexandra has taken a philosophical approach. "The 'worlds' are fair, for the most part," she says. "Tons of competitors quit because they feel disappointed by the judges. I believe everyone gets what they deserve - eventually."

"It's politics," Paul Orlando says. "Particularly at the highest level. There's nothing you can do about it, unfortunately. It's like ice skating, it's subjective."

Some have gone so far as to suggest rhythmic gymnastics should be dumped from the Olympics. There have been judging scandals in rhythmic gymnastics.

"The Olympic qualifiers are particularly competitive," Alex says. "Judges are always looking at the standings, throughout the season at every competition, so you want to do well all the time."

"You have to build a name, going in to the Olympics, as the judging is quite political," Marisa Orlando adds. "It's difficult to judge rhythmic gymnastics. One competitor is judged by 12 judges. There are four technical judges, four judges for execution, and four judges for artistry. Competitions are so close that a score of 0.1 makes a difference."

"At first, Alex fretted over the points judges gave her," her father says. "We told her to try to forget about it. If you go out there, do your thing, but the score isn't there, the judges still notice you, and it could affect the outcome next time or later on."

The Alexandra Orlando Rhythmic Gymnastics Quiz

Try this quiz and see how you score! Will you get bronze, silver, or gold?!

1. Mary Sanders' score for hoop at the Olympics was
a. remarkably low
b. protested by the USA
c. upheld by the FIG
d. all of the above

2. Victoria Orlando was named after
a. her uncles
b. her parents' love of winning
c. her grandfathers
d. none of the above

3. Lori Fung was
a. the first woman to win Olympic gold in rhythmic gymnastics
b. the first Canadian to win Olympic gold in rhythmic gymnastics
c. the first person on the planet to win Olympic gold in rhythmic gymnastics
d. all of the above

4. Alex's role model was
a. Camille Martens
b. Mary Sanders
c. Lori Fung
d. Erika-Leigh Stirton
e. all of the above

5. Mimi Masleva coached for
a. Bulgaria
b. Japan
c. China
d. Canada
e. USA
f. all of the above

6. The nickname Alex the Great was coined by
a. Melbourne newspapers
b. Australian media
c. Victoria Orlando
d. Paul Orlando
e. Marisa Orlando

7. A perfect score in rhythmic gymnastics would be
a. 100
b. 90
c. 80
d. 60

8. Rhythmic gymnastics was brought to Canada by
a. Annely Riga
b. Evelyn Koop
c. Dimitritchka Masleva
d. Anne Merklinger

9. At the Commonwealth Games, Alex
a. was the first woman to win six gold medals in rhythmic gymnastics
b. tied the record for most medals won by any athlete
c. was given the honour of being named Canada's flag-bearer
d. all of the above

10. In Canada, Alex was national senior champion in

a. 2003

b. 2004

c. 2005

d. 2006

e. all of the above

Answers

1. d   2. c   3. d   4. e   5. f   6. d   7. b   8. b   9. d   10. e

Your score:

9 or 10 = Gold

7 or 8 = Silver

5 or 6 = Bronze

1 to 4 = train harder at a higher level

Other Books by Martin Avery

- Northern Comfort
- Cottage Gothic
- First Impressions
- The Singing Rabbi
- Poetry Night In Canada (editor)
- Muskokans